CURRENT PERSPECTIVES ON AMERICAN LITERATURE

●POETRY ●FICTION ●DRAMA ●LITERARY THEORY

COMPARATIVE LITERATURE, CREATIVE WRITING AND MASS COMMUNICATION

S. PRAKASH RAO

ATLANTIC PUBLISHERS AND DISTRIBUTORS

Published by
ATLANTIC PUBLISHERS AND DISTRIBUTORS
B-2, Vishal Enclave, New Delhi-110 027.
Phones 5413460, 5429987

Sales Office
4346/4C, Ansari Road, Darya Ganj,
New Delhi-110 002.
Phones 3273880, 3285873
Fax 91-11-3285873

ISBN 81-7156-525-5

Typeset at
APD Computer Graphics, Delhi
Printed in India at
Fine Offset Press, Delhi-110 002.

Dedicated to

PROF. G. RAMI REDDY, CHAIRMAN, U.G.C.

ACKNOWLEDGEMENTS

I record my debt of gratitude to:

Prof. Darko Suvin, Prof. Leslie Fiedler, Prof. Isaac Sequeira, Prof. William Mulder and Prof. D.V.K. Raghavacharyulu for their unstinted cooperation and guidance.

To my teachers and well-wishers especially Prof. Chirantan Kulshresta and Prof. Malla Reddy, Vice-Chancellor, Osmania.

To the staff of American Studies Research Centre and USEFI.

To my parents, my wife Smt. P. Jahnavi and my daughter S. Sushma.

To the exciting world of ASRC.

To Shri G.K. Marar, Director, Doordarshan Kendra, Hyderabad.

PREFACE

AMERICAN LITERATURE is a preferred discipline of study in all Indian Universities. Despite the role of America as an Unipolar super power interfering in the destinies of developing countries, it enjoys the image of a Promised Land and hope for those who believe in liberalism, humanism, progressivism and democratic safeguards of human rights. These concepts are ingrained in the psyche and zeitgeist of the authors of American Classics. A student who initiates himself/herself into this exciting realm of intellectual mountaineering and scholarly and archival archaeology is at loss in the class room. This book seeks to provide fresh insights and current perspectives based on the generally accepted doctrines of American Studies. As a ''permanent fixture'' of American Studies Research Centre, Hyderabad, it is my pleasure to re-initiate, if not, reindoctrinate a scholar, into the world of Nineteenth and Twentieth Century American Literature.

I have adapted certain divergent questions relevant for applied Arts.

DR. S. PRAKASH RAO

CONTENTS

1. INTRODUCTION : NINETEENTH CENTURY POETRY IN AMERICA

Some of the best works of America were written during the 1840s and 1850s. They are :

- Tales of the Grotesque and Arabesque (1840)
- Essays (1840)
- The Scarlet Letter (1850)
- Walden (1851)
- Moby Dick (1851)
- Leaves of Grass (1855).

Some literary historians call this period "a flowering or Golden day or renaissance" of American Literature.

Edgar Allan Poe was the most influential author and artist of this period. His influence grew in Europe. Poe's briiliant poem *Eureka* (1847) was translated by Baudelaire without loosing the cosmological significance of the poem. Dostoievsky and French symbolists gave wide prominence to his works. Poe's detective stories were artistically and psychologically designed. Poe influenced Conan Doyle, Jules Verne and H.G. Wells. Poe was a forerunner of a style of writing which was later acclaimed only during the life and times of Hemingway. The main contributions of Poe may be outlined here:

- Poe contributed to the concept of autonomy of Art
- He influenced the Pre-Raphaelite movement
- He also influenced Painting, Music according to Mallarme.
- In *Eureka* he said:

  The plots of God are perfect.

  The Universe is a plot of God.

This means that art is self-contained.

- Poe contributed to the concept of Beauty in *The Poetic Principle*.

> Inspired by an ecstatic presence of the glorious beyond the grave, we struggle by multiform combinations among the things and thoughts of Time to attain a portion of that Loveliness whose very elements, perhaps, appertain to eternity alone. . . those divine and rapturous joys, of which through the poem or through the music, we attain to but brief and indeterminate glimpses.

The above statement may be described as a 19th century concept of creative process. Poe first propounded the theory of a poem for poem's sake and hence he came to advocate art for art's sake theory. He rejected a didactic poem.

– Poe advocated that Poetry ought to be a disclosure of Beauty.

Poe contributed to the concept of art which the new critics formulated later: that art should be self-contained.

William Bryant (1794-1878) contributed to the serene conception of death in *Thanatopsis* and the century concentrates on the theme of death in most of the writings. Emerson (1803-1882) contributed to the abstracting power and transcendental nature of the literature of the century. He offered the intellectual Declaration of Independence. Emerson's contribution can be epitomised :

- Emerson guided the two literary clubs: The Social Circle; The Transcendental Club.
- He contributed to Orientalism in American Litt.
- He made use of the literary tradition of Paradox.
- He freed the American verse from the tyranny of the metre and laid stress on the argument of the poem.
- He saved the U.S. from intellectual isolationism.
- Defined poetry as rhythmic creation of Beauty. Said that Poetry was a metre making argument. He popularised the transcendental beliefs:
    - The Over-soul pervades the Universe.
    - Underlining of unity in diversity of the Universe.
    - Faith in intuition rather than in understanding
    - Self-reliance is God-reliance
    - God is in all beings and substances
    - Modern man invades nature impiously for selfish reasons
    - divine inspiration is there in every work of art

– Emerson directed Thoreau (1817-1862) to the *Bhagavad Gita* and Oriental literature.

Another important poet of 19th century is Hawthorne (1804-1864). He stressed the fact that nobody can meddle in the life of another. He pointed out that the human condition is by nature imperfect. Dickinson brought in the metaphysical aspects about love and death. Her tragic vision, deeply introspective expression, witty and personal account of life brought credit to this genre. She brought in the rebellious and iconoclastic individualism to the fore.

Dickinson created poetry out of her isolated existence. She advocated the puritan theory of immortality of soul. She defined poetry in poetic terms:

– Poetry is a frostless garden.
– it is a lamp that burns on after Aladin is dead.
– it is a ballet.
– it is the truth to be achieved indirectly.
– it is magic.
– it is perfume.

These novel definitions attracted her poetry besides the dark themes in Literature. Her experiments in prosody and metre and other stylistic oddities attracted the attention of scholars all over the world. Lowell and Holmes later made the genre a medium of intense debate. The scene was ripe for the arrival of Whitman on the scene.

Whitman's contribution was nationalising the dream or myth of America. His poetry conspicuously dealt three themes:

(1) American Democracy and her people,

(2) poetry of senses,

(3) of death and immortality.

His poetry pointed out the defects in American polity. He euologised Abraham Lincoln and celebrated common citizens. He said:

In the labour of engines and trades,
  and the labour of fields,
  I find the developments,
And find the eternal meanings.

These lines from *A Song for Occupations* represent the 19th century America. All sections of the people find mention in his poetry. He elevated all sections of people as "divine average" and mentioned people engaged in such crafts as leather-dressing and so on:

I hear America singing, the varied
carols I hear;
Those of mechanics–each one singing his,
as it should be, blithe and strong,
The carpenter singing his. . .
The mason singing his. . .

He thus envisioned a pragmatic and successful America.

Though Whitman said " I celebrate myself and I sing myself", he sang about America and about entire humanity. He shaped the ideas of 19th century Democracy and advocated its use. It is not an exaggeration to state that literature from Poe to Whitman found culmination in his poetry. His radical view of Democracy with emphasis on equal rights and abolition of slavery, free trade, prison reform, and women's rights and above all abolitions of all monopolies established Democracy in America on firm footing. As a journalist he envisioned all these in *Democratic Vistas* (1817).

Nineteenth century poetry found in Whitman a mouthpiece of Democracy :

– a means of self-development
– rejecting hoggish materialism
– ever-modern dream of earth.

All these find expression in *Song of Myself*:

I dote on myself – there is that lot of me,
and all so luscious;
Each moment, and whatever happens, thrills me
with joy
O I am wonderful!

These lines are not indicative of self-glorification but of the Universal aspect realises in 19th century.

Questions

1. "Within but a decade the prophecies began to be fulfilled" – What were the prophecies of 19th century American Literature
2. How did Poe influence the literature of the period?

3. What are the aesthetic positions of writers of 19th century?
4. The poem is a self-contained work of Art. Explain with reference to the contexts of 19th century America and Europe.

References

1.	David Daiches	:	A History of English Litt.
2.	Barret Wendell	:	A Literary History of America
3.	H.M. Jones	:	Belief and Disbelief in American Literature
4.	Robert E Spiller	:	The Cycle of American Litt.
5.	V.S. Pinto	:	Crisis in English Poetry
6.	F.O. Matthiessen	:	American Renaissance
7.	Dr. Prakash Rao, S.	:	19th Century American Litt.
8.	Dr. Prakash Rao, S.	:	Current Issues in Litt.

For Creative Writing Course Students of IGNOU

– Attempt a literary history of 19th Century Hindi or Telgu Litt.
– Identify certain chief idiosyncratic tendencies in your regional litt.

2. EMERSON

I. THE AMERICAN SCHOLAR

Ralph Waldo Emerson (1803-1882) grew up in difficult financial circumstances. He lost his father at the age of eight and this perhaps explains his emphasis on self-reliance and moral uprightness. He was an odd-jobs-man at Harvard but managed to become a father of Divinity. He was a Pastor at Boston. He experienced many doubts regarding Church rituals such as the occurrence of the Lord's Supper. Many biographers overemphasize this point because he did not support many practices of the Church. He is reported to have said at a congregation :

> It is my desire, in the office of a Christian minister, to do nothing which I cannot do with my whole heart. Having said this I have said all. I have not got any hostility to this institution. I am only stating my want of sympathy with it.

He resigned his office as a clergyman in 1832. He was an "old, unbeatable Puritan stuff" and he went on the European tour to meet some leading Romantic writers of his times. He met Wordsworth, Coleridge and Carlyle. Back from this tour he settled at Concord and developed friendship with Thoreau, Hawthorne and other precursors of Transcendental thought. He published the famous Transcendental journal, *The Dial* and carried on the experiments in community living based on his understanding of Hindu settlements or Agraharas. All these facts are relevant to understand his concept of robust, self-reliant individualism. He published *Nature* (1836) which contained the most seminal ideas and reflections on spiritual aspects of Transcendentalism. He published *Essays* (1841) which contained his concept of the oversoul and Compensation besides Self-reliance. The only thing he could achieve by his addresses at Harvard was the antagonism of fellow divines. His spiritual, intuitive experiences were dubbed as unorthodox and heretical. However, by 1850 Civil War was rampant and he was recognised as an intellectual. Some radicals supported him and he supported the anti-slavery movement.

Preceding to the publication of *The American* Emerson delivered twelve lectures which were published as *The Philosophy of History*. *The American Scholar* was a lecture addressed by Emerson at Harvard *Lyceum* (Aristotle's Lecture Hall) called the Phi Beta Kappa Society in 1837. It is described as 'The Intellectual Declaration of Independence' and as a *magna carta* of American letters. In this he declares:

> our day of dependence, our long apprenticeship to
> the learning of other lands, draws to a close.

This line is self-explanatory. Emerson feels that the American scholars must stop imitating the European models and must depend upon their originality and intuitive perceptions. He addresses the American writers to use their native talents and herald a new cultural epoch. The Americans are free politically but are still in cultural chains of Europe. Even in matters of social and intellectual importance they were drawing their models from England. This slavish imitation is detrimental to the growth of intellectual movement in America.

Emerson later advocates his concept of man. According to him, there is a fable which mentions that Man was divided into several men only for his benefit. The fable circulates the notion that the hand is divided into fingers so that they are useful to the hand as well as to man. The entire society is for the benefit of Man. Society in turn is divided into several individuals and not communities so that they will nurture it. He says :

> The state of the Society is one in which the
> members have suffered amputation from the Truth,
> and strut about so many walking monsters–
> –a good finger, a neck, a stomach, an elbow
> but never man.

Man has become a fragmented entity and Society is a grotesque monster with all the limbs separated and claiming functional autonomy.

In order to integrate all these organs he advocates a process of integration. Three forces shape the character of the American Scholar:

1. nature,
2. the mind of the past, and
3. active life.

Nature is an active force shaping the awareness of the scholar. There is a close correlation between these two forces. Man experiences close correspondence between his mind and nature. Man perceives the interrelatedness of several objects of nature. Emerson concludes by saying that the laws of nature are the laws of soul of man. His soul is a manifestation of the Universal Soul. Nature and Soul are like the leaf and flower which come out of the same root. He says :

One is seal and one is print.

Emerson derives two maxims out of his observation of the inter-relatedness of nature and man:

1. Know thyself
2. Study nature.

These are revealed in the following lines:

> the ancient precept, "Know thyself" and the modern precept, "Study nature", become at last one maxim.

The mind of the past is contained in Literature, Art and institutions created by man. Classics influence the mind of a scholar and make him great. A great writer puts life into Truth and *vice versa*. Hence his perennial values influence not only his times but even the posterity is influenced. Books are the readymade sources for this purpose. He says:

> Books are the best of things,
> well used;
> abused, among the worst.

He cautions that the scholar must not blindly adhere to whatever the book says. He hates a book worm and welcomes a scholar who rejuvenates his own creativity with the help of a classic.

Emerson contradicts the popular notion that the scholar is a recluse and not a man of action. He firmly believes that only an activist could be a scholar and one must necessarily be. He must develop his contemplative and meditative nature. Experience is the raw material and intellect shapes out exquisite patterns and creations. In this context he makes two important statements:

> Thinking is the function.
> Living is the functionary.

These statements mean that a life of contemplation is essential for a man of action. It is a resource and shapes the character. He says:

Character is higher than intellect. The words of a man would reveal the weight of his experience. A hollow man is one who has no experience and hence his words sound hollow. He thinks that we can know "instantly" whose words are loaded with life and whose are not.

The American Scholar defines and mentions the traits of a genuine scholar. Emerson says that the scholar is a man of thought and one who lives through the process of contemplative and intuitive thinking. This concept is close to the Vedic concept of meditation. He says:

> He is the world's eye.
>
> He is the world's heart.
>
> He is to resist the vulgar prosperity that retrogrades ever to barbarism, by preserving and communicating heroic sentiments, noble biographies, melodious verse, and the conclusions of History. . . .

The above lines amply testify and reveal the duties and the responsibilities of a Scholar. Self-Trust is the foundation on which American Scholarship rests. He recalls his earlier experiences of segregation and isolation when he tried to lead his society. The scholar must interpret what is best in his culture and listen to the voice of reason. The conclusions of History must guide the scholar. This is helpful to guide the society he represents in turn; because, nature and past are the guiding forces of Character.

Questions

1. Discuss Emerson as a poet of man.
2. Analyse Emerson's emphasis on Scholarship.
3. Bring out the idealism in Emerson's concept of the American scholar.

References

1.	H.H. Waggoner	:	Emerson as Poet.
2.	Robert Spiller	:	The Literary History of the U.S.
3.	Dr. Prakash Rao, S.	:	The Restoration Drama.
4.	Dr. Prakash Rao, S.	:	Milton and Major Metaphysicals

II. EMERSON : THE AMERICAN SCHOLAR – *Contd.*

In the last unit you studied about certain biographical details of Emerson and the concepts in *The American Scholar*. In this unit I shall round-up the discussion on this subject and offer in a nutshell some concepts which are essential in understanding Emerson.

As a philosopher, Emerson preached the following maxims. Even in understanding this work these ideas will be of use in comprehending his vision and basic ideas:

1. Self-reliance
2. Religion of spirit.
3. God as law
4. The world as God's creation.
5. Man has the spark of divinity in him.

These ideas are central to his Poetry and crucial in understanding his philosophical standpoints about Man and his world.

1. Emerson uses the phrase self-reliance as synonymous with God-reliance. He means that man should be obedient to the Over-Soul. He must act according to the instincts of the Soul. He said:

> The unconscious is ever an act of God Himself.

This concept is a mixture of Mysticism and Puritanism. This is extended to the American scholar.

2. Emerson rebelled against the traditional interpretation of Religion and the Church. He said:

> The relations of the soul to the divine are so pure
> that it is profane to seek to interpose helps.

He believed that character makes the State unnecessary. His faith in America as a Promised Land further strengthened this belief of spirit.

3. As a Puritan he did not believe in idol or symbol to denote God. He saw God as a chief law giver like any other Puritan. So men should obey the Ten Commandments to seek Christian salvation. So respect for morality and law meant respect for God.

4. Like all religious thinkers Emerson believed that the World was an emanation from God. This belief was reinforced by his study of Indian mysticism. Why is the World affected by evil? (For Comparison q.v. : my book on *MILTON*).

> 1. Emerson believed that in "Nature all these disagreeable individuals integrate themselves into a clean and pleasing whole."
> 2. As a law of compensation "the intentions of Providence to limit human perfectibility and to blind together good and evil, like life and death, by indissoluble connections."

5. Indian classics strengthened his belief that man has the divine spark in him. He was particularly fond of the concept: *AHAM BRAHMASMIH*. Coleridge is credited with gifting this idea to Emerson besides the Indian metaphysical distinction between Reason and Understanding. He said:

> In all my lectures I have taught one doctrine namely, the infinitude of the private man.

Let us examine these basic tenets to *The American Scholar*.

The scholar represents these ideas and he should believe in the following maxim :

> to ignorance and sin, it is flint. They adopt themselves to it as they may; but in proportion as a man has anything in him divine, the firmament flows before him and takes his signet and form.

Emerson believed that fear flows out of ignorance and illiteracy. The scholar must mould the minds of the people. An ignorant man thinks that the world is like flint whereas the scholar thinks that it is malleable and plastic. This is because he knows that the world is animated by one Soul. This concept is clearly stated in the following lines :

> It is one light which beams out of thousand stars.
> It is one soul which animates all men.

So the scholar must perform a special role. He should lead the people in all walks of life. The scholar must note that the literature of the poor and the feelings of the child must be taken into account. The central focus of literature has changed from heroic aspects to these facts of everyday life.

The scholar must not follow whatever is blindly written. He must study during the 'intervals of darkness'. He says:

> the scholar is that man who must take up into himself all the ability of the time, all the contributions of the past, all the hopes of the future.

These lines tell us that he wants the scholar to be a dynamic activist. He should educate himself through nature. And reinforce his learning by books and by action. He should become the world's eye and make the world more authentic. Emerson dismissed the notion that the present age is an age of introversion. He does not find any symptom of sickness and excess thinking but the underdogs have found place in literature. He is against the genteel and aristocratic tradition of Europe. He is happy that :

> a nation of men will for the first time exist, because
> each believes himself inspired by the Divine Soul
> which also inspires all men.

These lines sum up his belief in men and self-confidence.

To conclude, the American Scholar must have the following qualities:

1. self-confidence
2. self-trust
3. self-sufficiency
4. self-dependent
5. leadership
6. individualism
7. divine soul
8. bravery
9. of universal mind
10. obedience to over-soul

These qualities are discussed in proper contexts and hence the essay is called as the intellectual declaration of independence for America and by implication to all men of letters.

Questions

1. The American Scholar is an intellectual declaration of independence. Discuss.
2. What are the qualities of the Scholar?
   In what way they are different from the Puritan standpoint.

References

1. Clement Wood : Poets of America
2. F.O. Matthiessen : American Renaissance.

Comparative Studies

For a fuller discussion on the crucial concepts please refer to my book :

ELIOT INFOTECH : A TEACHER'S MANUAL

III. EMERSON : THE CRITIQUE

A critique is a collection of criticism on a particular topic. In this unit you will learn about various views and approaches of various critics and critcasters on Emerson, in general, and The American Scholar in particular.

Willis Wager, in his *American Litt: A World View*, observes:

> Between 1830 and 1860, if ever, rose our Wattses, Addisons, Homers. The quarter century before the Civil War was the period of American Literary classics–a flowering or golden day or renaissance. It was a distinct era in world literature, like that of Periclean Athens, Augustan Rome, Elizabethan England, or Louis XIV's Versailles.

Wager is estimating Emerson as a product of the above period, and as one of the inheritors of the legacy of "'New England Brahmins'." Such a view has obvious limitations because Emerson did not reflect a conservative theology like Anne Bradstreet, but evolved his own theory of Spirituality that is open-ended. He has entered in his ship diary on way to Europe :

> What under the Sun canst thou do then,
> pale face?
>
> Truly not much, but I can hope.

Wager makes another observation:

> In contrast to a Poe work, an Emerson Essay is usually an ascending spiral of increasing amplitude and abstraction. Basically the form is oratorical, for many of the essays are reworked lectures–often ending with peroration.

This is true of *The American Scholar*.

Emerson felt that man can only have second hand relationship with nature and God. Even the Scholar is incapable of having the direct relationship and communion. Wager asks the question: Why not a first hand one? He is right. In *Nature* (1836) Emerson says that nature is useful, has commodity uses, is beautiful, serves as a basis of language and has several disciplinary values. The following passage serves as a tool to understand his vision:

– As a plant upon the earth, so a man rests upon the bosom of God;
– he is nourished by unfailing fountains, and draws at his need inexhaustible power.
– Who can set bounds to the possibilities of man?
– Once inhale the upper air, being admitted to behold the absolute natures of justice and Truth, and we learn that man has access to the entire mind of the Creator, is himself the creator in the finite.

These lines should answer the controversy created by Wager and others who consider that Edgar Allan Poe had more comprehensive view of man, scholar and nature than Emerson.

The Scholar is simply the man thinking. Emerson is said to have made 'this secular evocation of the old plain style sermon. . . digging at roots of Christian emotion and vision deep in the New England Soul.' Some critics think that 'it is a coherent formulation of an ideal for American scholarship different from the German one then being domesticated at Harvard'. The following passage is isolated for the didactive turbulence in Emerson:

> if the single man plant himself indomitably on his instincts, and there abide, the huge world will come round to him. Patience – patience; and for solace the perspective of your own infinite life; and for work the study and communication of principles, the making those instincts prevalent, the conversion of the world. . .
>
> A nation of men will for the first time exist, because each believes himself inspired by the Divine Soul which also inspires all men.

This passage has all the attributes of a sermon. Emerson found British writing 'utilitarian and insular'. Dickens "writes London tracts", Macaulay teaches the merit of modern philosophy "is to avoid ideas and avoid morals". Wager interprets this criticism as follows :

> To Emerson the purpose of literature is no more *of this world* than it is to Poe – though Emerson would grant it a more overtly didactic aim.

This is a valid justification. Emerson declared that "I am, in all my theory, ethics, and politics a poet". He believed in writing original and archetypal ideas as the poem 'Bacchus' testifies. His interest in Vedas is reflected in 'Brahma':

> If the red slayer think he slays,
> Or if the slain think he is slain,
> They know not well the subtle ways
> I keep, and pass, and turn again.

These lines bring us to Emerson's Orientalism. Critics quote the following lines to prove that he thought Asia was 'spiritually more vigorous than Europe'. He says:

> By the law of contraries, I look for an irresistible taste for Orientalism in Britain. For a self-conceited modish life, made up of trifles, clinging to a corporeal civilization, hating ideas, there is no remedy like the Oriental largeness. That astonishes and disconcerts English decorum. For once, there is thunder it never heard, light it never saw, and power which trifles with time and space.

This appreciation for the land of Himalayas inspired T.S. Eliot and he acknowledged the same in *The Waste Land*. Emerson went further and asserted :

> It is the surest sign of national decay, when the Brahmins can no longer read or understand the Brahminical philosophy.

Read with the concepts we dealt about *The American Scholar*, these lines indicate that he wanted the spiritualists to play the role of the Scholar. This is because, like poets, they stand "among partial men for the complete man, and apprise us not of his wealth, but of common wealth". Arnold considered Emerson's essays 'the most important prose work of the century'. Froude, Tyndall and Nietzsche found in his writings a 'prefigurations of their own thoughts. Emerson deeply influened the leaders in India. The following are the aspects that influenced the intellectual leaders in India and all over the world:

Emerson as a transcendentalist

Emerson belonged to the group of transcendentalists comprising of :

- Margaret Fuller
- W.H. Channing
- Thoreau

His transcedentalism was a result of the influences of :

- Plato and Neo-platonists like Plotinus
- Romantics like Coleridge and Carlyle
- Oriental mysticism

The beliefs of all of the above mentioned scholars are reflected in his poems and in the concept of the Scholar.

The following are some of the transcendental beliefs of Emerson:

1. Optimism and confirmed idealism to the core.
2. Belief in the supremacy of God as the creator.
3. Belief in Over-soul.
4. Hindu belief that every object has life in it. Even the inanimate have a reason to exist.
5. Man incorporates divinity in him.
6. Man and nature are closely related.
7. Central ideas of *Brahma* based on *Geeta*, the poem *Sphinx* voice his beliefs on eternity and timelessness.
8. The inevitability of death, and its means to a new life of spirit *e.g.: Threnody & The Rhodora*
9. Feeling sensuous in the presence of Beauty :
   e.g. Woodnotes, Blight, Give all to Love.
10. Art is divinely inspired.

(All these points are not fully discussed here because they are partly essential for understanding of the piece prescribed and for an overall impression of the author).

Emerson as a Teacher or Moral and Didactic Element in His Writings

It is not possible to comprehend any work of the Emerson canon without considering him as a teacher. The following are some considerations :

1. His guidelines to Americans regarding the Scholar.

2. His preachings regarding inculcation of spiritualism and reduce materialism.
3. His narratorial voice and tone as an "Indian mystic".
4. Condemnation of war against Mexico – *e.g.* Ode to W.H. Channing.

Emerson's Stress on Intuition

The poem *Uriel* is partly autobiographical and illustrates his theory on Intuition. It is the method of transcendentalists and use of logic to comprehend divine truths is forbidden. He called it 'hobgoblin of little minds' and did not care for consistency for its own sake.

It fell in the ancient periods
  which the brooding soul surveys
or ever the wild Time coined itself
  Into calendar months and days. . .

The heretical ideas of Emerson are expressed in above lines.

Another dimension of Emerson that must be mentioned here is his respect for voice of God. The Scholar is often directed to act intuitively and also behave like any other transcendentalist. He can lead his fellow men only if he listens to this voice of God. This is also essential for the scholar to be self-reliant. He expressed these ideas as follows :

Henceforth, please God, forever I forego
The yoke of men's opinions, I will be
Light-hearted as a bird, and live with God.

These ideas are similar to those of Kant and Plato. He also voiced the ideas of St. Paul who believed in seeking and finding for a life full of evangelism and practicable hope. As nature-mystic he used the words, beauty, commodity, and discipline for nature. Contemporary environmentalists will find more material in Emerson's work than people of any age. Nature meant to him the evidence of perennial circulation of divine love. The American scholar must be able to appreciate this periphery of Pantheistic notion. Emerson further stated that nature with all her elements can be the medium to bring men close to the Universe.

Critical Appreciation of Emerson's Works and Art

All told, Emerson is controversial and stimulating. His reputation rests as a transcendentalist, as an Orientalist mystic and as a champion of intellectual independence. In 1847 he created a storm in the critic's circles by his act of renouncing, preaching and his heretical views on Christ and Christianity. Indian contribution to Emerson's studies is one of appreciation and at times smacks of sentimentality.

The first criticism about his views is that mostly it is unreliable and impracticable. Arnold rated his prose as original but disclaimed his poetry by saying that he was not a legitimate poet. Eliot who followed him also considered Emerson as naive and artificial. The New Critics who followed Eliot also did not consider him as a true poet solely on the basis that he does not voice the ambiguities and ironies of life.

A balanced critic like Yvor Winters noticed dangerous sentimentality, lack of regard for tradition and authority in his works.

All these critics have been called as detractors by some admirers of Emerson. Tyndall called him a noble soul and religiously studied and recited his poetry which undoubtedly reflects deep religiosity. He is profound though certain technical faults could be noticed. The mystical element nullifies all the prejudicial and biased judgments. If he was not a poet, he was a revealer and his revelations make him true aesthetician.

Emerson did not train his ear for verse rhythms. Like a prophet he erred in some places but those ideas were well-received. There is still no agreement regarding the quality of his poetry. Emerson declared that : 'I am a bard least of bards'. But the chief interest in the study of Emerson and Thoreau, is about their transcendentalism and their vision of things.

Questions

1. What according to Emerson are the qualities of the American scholar?
2. Consider 'The American Scholar' as America's literary independence.
3. Bring out the mystical and transcendental beliefs of Emerson from the work you have studied.
4. What does Emerson say about the Europeans?
5. Emerson is a noble soul. Justify.
6. Emerson is not a legitimate artist. Refute the argument citing from the texts prescribed for you.
7. Emerson's idealism is theoretical.

References

1. Willis Wager : American Litt: A World View.
2. W.P. Trent : A History of American Litt.

3. F.E. Matthiessen : American Renaissance.
4. O.W.Holmes : Emerson.

Comparative Litt.

1. Compare Emerson's Transcendentalism with that of Ramakrishna, Viswanatha Satyanarayana.
2. Compare Emerson's mysticism with that of Eliot's orientalism – Dr. SPR
3. Compare Emerson's use of *Suggestion* with Puttanna Kanagal's technique.

*

3. E.A. POE

I. *THE RAVEN*

Poe (1809-1849) was a true artist who made an indelible impression on American literary scene though his work and mission were incomplete. He is remembered for all that is ghastly and gothic, the traumatic and turbulent aspect of things. He perfected the art of expressing such things in a style that is inimitable and haunting. He was the father of a new genre of writing called the Detective fiction and thrillers. He is an acknowledged master of weaving romantic charm and beauty and vivid character into a tension-filled atmosphere. His childhood was traumatic and had all the troubles of orphan upbringing.

Poe began his literary career as a Satirist, while at Manor House School, London. He was called as ''self-willed, capricious, inclined to be imperious, and. . . not steadily kind or even amiable'', by his aristocratic friends. He nurtured horrific and grotesque imagination right from childhood with precocious talents. He joined army and was still writing poems. His life was full of romantic misadventures and his poor background was blamed every time. These biographical details probably explain the solitude, despair and penury of his fiction such as ''MS Found in a Bottle''. His genius was recognized when he served as a literary Editor for several magazines. *The Raven & Other Poems* was published in 1840. In the same year Poe published *Tales of Grotesque and Arabesque*. To the reading public it was a declaration of the central principle of his artistry and fantastic fiction. As a magazinist he was a success but he yearned for commercial success that has been eluding for ever.

Arthur Quinn wrote a critical biography of Poe in 1941 and countered the criticism of Eliot. Eliot described the writings of Poe as ''slipshod'' (though he was influenced) and a host of Poe detractors called his writing obscurantist, rough and crude. Shaw, Paul Valery acclaimed Poe's fictional and critical writings. Scholars have summed up his life as a study 'in insecurity, instability and frustration'. His literary executor, Rufus Griswold, defamed Poe after his death and created an image of Poe as a psychological monster wanting in morals. This was later proved false.

Poe's works clearly demonstrate a working of the genius. In about fifty poems he exemplified a poetic theory, experimented with the figures of speech and tried to create an atmosphere of *Son et lumier* (sight and sound) Emerson uncharitably called him a 'jingleman'. Poe elevated American criticism and pointed out certain plagiarisms of great writers. He perfected the neglected field of short story and made a pre-established design compulsory for such creative minds.

A brief review of some patent poems of Poe and his theory of Poetry, his concept of poetic imagination, his aggrandisement of Beauty and its linkages to Truth are essential to understand a complex poem like *The Raven*.

The first poem *Sonnet* (1829) lamented about the dangers of military science. *Helen* (1831) celebrated ideal Beauty and Love with classical allusions and was followed by *Israfel* (1831) with full of cosmic imagery, verse effect, concentration of mood and atmosphere which are characteristic of Poe. *The Raven* appeared in 1845 and was famous for its methodical exposition. Several other poems like *Ulalume* (1847) took up themes such as the conflict between psyche and the body. The current day Psi-fi (Psychological branch of Science Fiction) seem to draw heavily from the poetics of *Eureka* (1848). The subject-matter of this poem is the cosmic unity of the Universe. Truly a jingleman cannot weave such dream fantasies !

Textual study of *The Raven*

The opening lines of the poem are the student's narration of the happenings of a bleak December night :

Once upon a midnight dreary, while I
    pondered, weak and weary,
Over many a quaint and curious volume of forgotten
    lore –
While I nodded, nearly napping, suddenly there
    came a tapping,
As of some one gently rapping, rapping, at
    my chamber door,

These lines describe the setting or the atmosphere which is crucial to the poem. The narrator was reading ancient books of magic though he was weak and tired. He was drowsy and half-asleep when he heard the gentle rapping. He thought some visitor is tapping at his door at this unearthly hour. The last line 'only this and nothing more' is significant in the context of the poem.

The bleakness of the atmosphere is gradually intensified with the suggestion of the embers of charcoal falling on the ground like ghost. The narrator waited for the next morning to arrive so that he could drown his sorrows in the study of books. He wanted to suppress his grief of loss of his beloved called Lenore. She was a "rare and radiant maiden whom the angels name Lenore". She is now dead and she is nameless forever. The poet suggests bleak melancholy and drowsiness in these lines:

For the rare and radiant maiden whom the
    angels name Lanore –
Nameless here for evermore.

The following lines are poetic and suggest his conception of versification :

And the silken, sad, uncertain rustling
    of each purple curtain
Thrilled me–filled me with fantastic
    terrors never felt before;
So that now, to still the beating of
    my heart, I stood repeating,
'Tis some visitor entreating entrance at
    my chamber door–

These lines create strange and mysterious fears felt by the narrator and induce the same in the mind of the readers. He was consoling himself and thought that it must be a late visitor. His soul grew stronger and he did not hesitate any longer. He opened the door and begged to be excused for opening the door so late. There was none and he only saw darkness and nothing more. He peered deep into darkness and stood there for long with fear and wonder. He was also doubting, dreaming dreams no living person ever dared to dream. He only witnessed unbroken silence and the stillness which did not give him any clue of the gentle tapping of the door. These lines create the strong suggestion or *Dhwani*, if you like, to the readers to indicate the fact that some supernatural presence might be there. This effect, which the modern Films have exploited, is called the Gothic effect which Poe delighted to create at every given context in his works, whether they are poems or stories. *The Fall of the House of Usher* is replete with such gothic utterances and suggestions. The voice thought :

Lenore –
This I whispered, and an echo murmured
back the word,
Lenore!
Merely this and nothing more.

He whispered Lenore thinking that she might have come as a spirit and tapping his door but he only heard his voice and nothing more. So decided to unravel the mystery with a burning soul. He heard a louder sound and he opened the window. It was the wind and nothing more. So he gained the composure of his heart.

When he opened the window a raven flirting and fluttering stepped in. It was a stately Raven of ancient times. Without hesitation he perched upon the statue of Athene, the Greek goddess of wisdom. He did nothing more. He calls this an ebony bird with a stern and dignified look. He was a horrid grave and primitive raven. This ugly, ominous bird repeated only never more. The narrator slipped into the realm of fancy to decode the meaning of the utterance of the bird. He called the bird Prophet of Doom and an Agent of evil sent by Satan. After a good deal of imploring the scholar said :

Be that word our sign of parting,
bird or fiend! I shrieked upstarting–

Again the bird replied 'never more'.

The raven is sitting still on the pale bust of Athene in his chamber. His eyes are full of demon's fire and you can see his shadow created by the lamp. The narrator says that his soul can never lift itself from the shadow on the floor. He repeats: never more.

The poet successfully creates a deep effect unprecedented in Poetry. He gradually moves from anticipation to suspense. Later on this shift of focus is from sudden consternation to unexpected irony. The bird challenges his weird imagination. The narrative structure of the poem is as follows:

The student --

– evolution of atmosphere – despair.

— fantastic terror.

The raven – never more

The situation – 1. surcease of sorrow

2. poignancy

3. mystery of the visitor
4. psychological tension and intensification of despair.

The questions: What is the msytery of the bird?

Is there any possibility of relief from pain?

Questions : when the bird plays the role of a prophet and the gloomy mood converges on the bird:

– Is there no hope after death?
– Is there any form of sentience after death?
– Is there loss of my identity?
– Does escape have an ethical angle?

The spectrum of darkening mood can be summed up in the form of a black-board summary, for your easy recapitulation and recall:

1. first sets the mental reaction going on to a crescendo
2. repeats meaninglessly
3. mystery is added to meaninglessness.
4. degree of excitement (Stanza 10)
5. intensifies sorrow (Stanzas, last three)
6. intensifies terror and psychic paralysis.

The mood: the sorrow, the mystery and the terror.

The raven's course :

1. starts as a bird of refuge
2. becomes a mysterious object
3. deepens mystery with never more
4. endows depressing personality
5. a prophet/thing of evil
6. a shadow, insubstantial but formidable.

I have tried to simplify the narrative structure for easy comprehensive because the poem was revised 16 times for creating an organic work of art.

The chief points about the poem are :

1. its brilliant narrative structure
2. its conversational tone
3. its dramatization of despair

4. its capacity to induce the feeling
5. its portrayal of abnormal reaction to sorrow as self-torture.

There is a poem by name Lenore wherein the details are given about her. She is a young and beautiful lady but awaiting death. Her body is described as golden and her soul saintly.

This poem is remarkable for its craftsmanship, art and its ability to make effect. It was an instant success and had mixed reaction in the beginning. It is a good example of the art and craft of composition as enunciated by Poe. Poe's important contributions to the field of criticism are:

1. The Philosophy of Composition
2. The Poetic Principle.

Questions

1. Attempt a critical appreciation of The Raven.
2. What is the central idea of The Raven?
3. Discuss the theme and technique of The Raven.
4. Poe is a poet of Love and Beauty – Justify this statement with your analysis of the poem *The Raven*.

References

1. E.H. Davidson, Poe : A Critical Study.
2. L. Fiedler : Love and Death in the American Novel.

II. THE PHILOSOPHY OF COMPOSITION

The Philosophy of Composition is a seminal work of literary criticism in American Litt. It states Poe's theories on many matters of fundamental importance. Poe initiates discussion on plot in Dicken's novel and says that :

> Nothing is more clear than that every plot, worth the name, must be elaborated to its *denouement* before anything be attempted with the pen.

This statement questions the notions of divine inspiration or emotions recollected in tranquility or any other matter which is considered to be product of original imagination. He further elaborates this point:

> It is only with the denouement constantly in view that we can give a plot its indispensable air of consequences, or causation, by making the incidents, and especially the tone at all points, tend to the development of the intention.

Poe addressed himself to the fundamentals of the creative process, its role and effect on the society. He was frank and forthright in his assertions. He thought there was a radical error in the 'usual mode of constructing a story'.

About the effect Poe says it should be considered immediately after the novel has been thought off. He says that "Most writers–poets in especial–prefer having it understood that they compose by a species of fine frenzy–and ecstatic intuition–and would positively shuddering at letting the public take a peep behind the scenes, all the elaborate and vacillating crudities of thought–at the true purpose seized only at the last moment. . ." He illustrates the point by citing *The Raven* and says :

> It is my design to render it manifest that no one point in its composition is referable either to accident or intuition–that the work proceeded step-by-step to its completion with the precision and rigid consequence of a mathematical problem.

Poe does not believe in the circumstances that lead to creative process. According to him inspiration is not a catalyst in the creative process and it is sheer hypocrisy to talk about it. He points out that his celebrated poem *The Raven* is thoroughly artificial and a product of deliberate effort. Such a view contradicts the position maintained by several classical and romantic writers.

I now quote Poe's ideas on other resources that creatives employ and later examine his standpoints from the angle of aesthetics:

On Intention

If any literary work is too long to be read at one sitting, we must be content to dispense with the immensely important effect derivable from unity of impression – for if two sittings are required, the affairs of the world interfere. . .

On long poem

> What we term a long poem is, in fact merely a

succession of brief ones–that is to say, of brief poetical effects.

On limits

there is a distinct limit, as regards length, to all works of literary art–the limit of a single sitting.

On choice of Impression

the design of tendering the work...

(must be) universally appreciable...

Beauty is the sole legitimate province of the poem.

On Beauty

That pleasure which is at once the most intense, the most elevation, and the most pure, is, I believe... is found in the contemplation of the beautiful.

On Tone

is the highest manifestation (of Beauty)
Beauty of whatever kind, its supreme development, invariably excites the sensitive soul to tears. Melancholy is thus the most legitimate of all the poetical tones.

Poe illustrates these points citing extensively from *The Raven*. He proves it as a poem of excellence and that it is possible to write a poem without inspiration. He combined in it "two ideas, of a lover lamenting his deceased mistress and a Raven continuously repeating the word 'never more'." The rhythm or metre of this poem is trochaic and octameter acatalectic, alternating with heptametre cataletic. He also paid attention to locale and decide on close circumscription of space : the chamber. He employed contrast and built an air of the fantastic.

Poe skilfully handles his subject in *The Raven* and the poem remains one of the best poems with a remarkable denouement, and richness. He makes the raven emblematical of 'mournful and never ending remembrance'. This poem can also be interpreted from the point of view of *The Poetic Principle*, which elevates Poe to the level of Coleridge. In this he clearly says :

I hold that a long poem does not exist. . .
Along poem is simply a flat contradiction in terms.

Poe is against "undue brevity (as it) degenerates into mere epigrammatism". He declares that "the ultimate object of all Poetry is Truth. Every poem, it is said, should inculcate a moral; and by this moral is the poetical merit of the work to be adjudged". But besides this, Poe says:

> Dividing the world of mind into its three most obvious distinctions, we have the Pure intellect, Taste, and Moral sense.

He says that taste is judged by the sense of the beautiful. It is the supernal Loveliness and the poetic sentiment may develop into various models such as Painting and Sculpture. He goes on to define poetry as "words as the Rhythmical creation of Beauty". And its sole arbiter is Taste.

The poetic principle of Poe is "the human Aspiration for Supernal Beauty, the manifestation of the Principle is always found in an elevating excitement of the Soul–quite independently of that passion which is the intoxication of the Heart–or of that Truth which is the satisfaction of the Reason." He distinguishes two types of Love:

1. the true, the divine Eros–the Uranian
2. the purest and the truest of all poetic themes: Dionaean Venus.

Having discussed Poe's own statements in the two critical writings we can attempt now to consider his theories on various subjects:

Poe's Theory of Poetry

It is said that Poe correlates poetry with music as he defines it as "The Rhythmical Creation of Beauty." Hence he desires the employment of :

1. refrain
2. jingling
3. rhymes
4. alliteration
5. assonance
6. melancholic tone.

This theory reveals that Poe was largely influenced by Kant. This makes it narrow in scope and ambiguous. He further believed in making a poem mechanical and devoid of personal and private experiences to make it universally acceptable. Some critics think that he developed this theory out of animosity and bickerings with some writers. He modified his views according to Editors.

Poe adopted his critical stances of Coleridge and rejected morality as basis of Poetry. Arnoldians naturally disapprove of this argument. He insisted Music and Death as definite subjects of Poetry but that would make Literature monotonous.

Poe's Critical Theory

Poe believed that the principle of writing depended upon the writer's conscious efforts. He agreed with the Transcendentalists of New England that the True or Beautiful are one and the same. Yvor Winters attacked Poe by saying that his poetry does not distinguish between Truth and Beauty. He wanted all Poems to be read in one sitting and that all poetry must excite the soul. Brevity for Poe produces the effect.

But in making Taste essential for Poetry Poe has advocated a theory of *Rasa* which has been developed by aestheticians of India, particularly the Sanskrit poets. The poetic aesthetic of Poe, if we can coin one such phrase, consists of length, beauty, melancholy and in so doing he is underscoring the fundamental aspects of creativity.

Questions

1. Critically appreciate Poe's theory of poetic composition.
2. Compare and contrast Poe's theories with those of Coleridge.
3. Write an Essay on Poe as a Critic.
4. Write Short Notes on:
   (a) denouement in Poetry
   (b) Beauty and Truth in Poetry
   (c) Tone in the Poem *The Raven*
   (d) The poetic principle.
5. Poetry should excite the soul. Discuss.
6. Do you agree with the analysis and justification of Poe on *The Raven*? Give Reasons.
7. What is the place of morality in Poetry according to Poe?

References

1. Richard Wilbur : Poe

2. Lewis Chase : Poe and His Poetry
3. D.M. Rein : Poe:The Inner Pattern
4. Perry Miller : The Transcendentalists
5. Robert Regan ed. : Poe: Twentieth Century Views
6. Arthur Ransome : Poe: A Critical Study
7. Dr. Prakash Rao, S. : Apocalyptic Vision in Modern American Fiction (ICAS/ASRC)

Comparative Studies

– Compare Poe's concepts of Creative Process with those of Wordsworth, Coleridge and Eliot.

4. EMILY DICKINSON

I. STUDY OF HER POETRY

Emily Dickinson (1830–1886) was mostly educated at home at Amherst. Her only companion was her father's clerk, Benjamin Newton. This explains her sense of withdrawal and isolation in her life. She was terribly shaken after her father's death. In 1853, her only masculine contact, a friend and possibly a guide, Benjamin died. These developments are highlighted by her biographers. The point here is that biographical criticism dominates in the analysis of Art and Poetical personality of Dickinson.

Amherst was a small town, but was quiet thickly-wooded area of the Connecticut metropolis. It was eighty miles away from Boston and Cambridge. Her father was the treasurer of the college and a leading citizen of the town. She was unaffected by the Civil war. She was secluded and liked to meet her sister Lavinia, her maid and Austin's family. She was always dressed in white. She was probably guilty of her slight figure, was reticent and avoided photographers. Some biographers attribute this indifference to her lack of good features. She was reckless as far as her creativity is concerned. She scribbled on whatever she could lay her hands on. But only Seven out of 1700 poems were printed anonymously. Those who claim to have seen her at her age of forty say:

> a little plain woman with two smooth bands of
> reddish hair and a face. . .with no good features.

She liked to read Bryant, Emerson and Lowell. These details are given to introduce the poetess but let me remind you that biographical criticism is long discarded and only Practical or aesthetic or psychological criticism are valid approaches to her criticism.

Another point the biographers point out is her jinxed love with Charles Wadsworth, a clergyman who was already married and settled at Philadelphia. This brought out emotional trauma. Her mother was paralysed a year after her father's death in 1874. These details are cited to explain the sense of anguish and depression in her poetry.

Emily did not approve of the publication of the poems in her life time; Lavinia sent a bunch of her sister's poems after her death to Thomas Higginson, the Editor of the *Atlantic Monthly*. She was a private poet and was not interested in publishing her poems. Some critics feel that she was an immature and a secluded person, with self-realization. She was recognized as a major poet only since 1920s. The image of an eccentric spinster has stuck to her.

As a poet she exhibited the following characterstics:

1. natural feelings
2. themes of hope, fear, time, etc.
3. paradoxical personality
4. imperfect rhyme-schemes
5. poetic conceits in the manner of Donne
6. Emersonian sense of harmony in nature
7. mystic poetic genius
8. ironic vision
9. individualism
10. death-obsession or "graveyardism"
11. extreme iconoclasm
12. pleasure-pain antithesis.

Emily Dickinson as a Puritan

Her attitude to Love, death and God establish her as a Puritan. Critics have estimated Dickinson as a reclusive and conservative person. Probably, she was a puritan by choice and circumstance. She was influenced by Emerson and Thoreau and she carried the doctrine of self-reliant individualism too far. Some critics call this attitude Emersonian self-possession. But there is also evidence to suggest that she did not accept the puritanical notion of God. In a poem "Drowning is not so Pitiful" she says "the Maker's cordial visage/However, good to see/ Is shunned, we must admit it/ Like an adversity." She sometimes calls God as a "father, banker or even a burglar." The one point of accepting death as the ultimate goal of life in a fatalistic manner recalls her puritanical bias. She might not be a Calvinist and her transcendentalism regards every other consideration as perjury. The following aspects reveal her regard for the teachings of Emerson and Thoreau :

- Conscience as a forum of self-reliance.
- maintaining inner purity.

Metaphysical tendencies in Emily Dickinson's Poetry

Dickinson's ambivalent puritanical stances force us to identify metaphysical tendencies in her poetry. There are some similarities with the conceits of Donne. Her speculations have been metaphysical and she relies more on introspection. Time, Life, Eternity and Death are the subject-matters of her poetry. She believes in using epigrammatic symbols such as 'veil your deathless tree'. She also employed certain metaphysical expressions:

My life closed twice before its close;
It yet remains to see
If immortality unveil
A third event to me,

Critics are quick to point out the poetic licence availed of by Emily in respect of grammar and rhythm. It is difficult to say whether she imitated Donne or Whitman as Higginson thought.

The transcendental aspects in her poetry refer to her ironic, tragic vision and her pre-occupation with the ultimate. She was concerned with understanding the meaning and purpose of the Universe and man's role in it.

Dickinson as a Mystic and Nature Poet

Dickinson was basically a mystic and a nature poet. Some oppose this idea and call her frame of mind as domestic and even whimsical. This is grossly unfair. In the poem "Behind Me–Dips Eternity" she says :

Behind me–dips Eternity–
Before Me–immortality–
Myself–the Term between–
Death but the Drift of Eastern Gray.

In "I Felt A Funeral, in My Brain" she says:

And then a Plank in Reason, broke
And dropped down, and down –
And hit a World, at every plunge
And Finished knowing–then–

The above lines are certainly mystic and transcendental. In "A Light Exists in Spring" she says :

A light exists in Spring

Not present on the Year
At any other period–
When March is scarcely.here

These lines establish her as much more than a nature's poet.

Dickinson thus exhibits mixed elements as a poet of 19th century America. That is why she is bracketed with Poe and Whitman as an exponent of all that 19th century America symbolised. Her lyrical style and intensely passionate spiritual experiences and a vision which is at once transcendental and mystic baffled her readers. She never wrote them with an eye on seeing them in print or make money or reputation. She was a private poet and hence she must be taken as a sincere poet with integrity and vision.

Questions

1. Consider Emily Dickinson as a poet of nature.
2. Discuss the theme and technique of any two poems you have studied.
3. Emily Dickinson is truly a lyric poet. Justify.
4. Write a note on the Art and poetic personality of Emily Dickinson.
5. Critically appreciate Dicknson's treatment of Nature in her poetry.
6. Write an essay on Emily Dickinson and her early influences.
7. The achievement of Emily Dickinson is remarkable. Substantiate.

References

1. Douglas Duncan : Emily Dickinson
2. George F. Whitcher : This was a Poet
3. David Daiches : Emily Dickinson
4. Richard Chase : Emily Dickinson
5. Dr. Prakash Rao, S. : "Current Issues in American Litt."

Comparative Studies

Compare Dickinsons's concepts with those of Donne.

II. TEXTUAL STUDY OF THE POEMS PRESCRIBED

1. *After Great Pain a Formal Feeling Comes*

This poem is considered to be a most remarkable poem of Dickinson as it is representative of the poet's characteristics as a metaphysical and lyric poet with a tragic vision. The opening lines of the poem indicate the inevitable nature of pain:

After great pain, a formal feeling comes
The nerves sit ceremonious, like Tombs –
The stiff Heart questions was it He,
that bore,
And yesterday, or Centuries before?

These lines reveal the end of pain after death. The poem consists of three stanzas which mimic the funeral rites after death. Death is the greatest obsession for Dickinson and she never lets her idea go astray from the thoughts of death. Its companion poem is "I felt a Funeral in my Brain." In the second stanza the poet says :

The feet mechanical, go round –
Of Ground, or Air, or Ought –
A wooden way
Regardless grown
A quartz contentment, like a stone –

The parts of the body have become independent and the nerves sit ceremonious. The feeling of the death is suggested here. She uses the symbols of lifelessness to suggest the quartz contentment or like stone which is a stage after suffering. The pain is not physical but mental because the nerves are like the mourning people. The image of the tomb reinforces our earlier impression of the funeral rites. The image of the poem suggests all the feelings of numbness, stillness and lifelessness. Christ has experienced the pain and suffering centuries before. The numbness does not suggest whether the Crucifixion has occurred yesterday or centuries before. This is because the humanity which constantly bore the pain and suffering has become inevitable part of it. This is the suggestion of the Heart. The appropriateness of the word quartz contentment lies in its suggestion of stony numbness and death. It suggests the crystallization of the feeling of numbness.

The theme of the poem is pain accompanied by death. The ironical use of the word ceremonious to suggest the funeral rites is apt. The last line of the poem sums up the poet's argument. The interlocking of images in this poem recalls the conceits employed by Donne. But Donne is explicit in his statement whereas she is implicit. The rhyme scheme of the poem is iambic pentametre with rhyming couplets.

2. ***I heard a fly buzz when I died***

This is a poem with death as its central theme. The opening lines describe the sensations of death and suffering :

> I heard a Fly buzz–when I died–
> The stillness in the Room
> Was like the stillness in the Air–
> Between the Heaves of Storm –

The stillness in the room is sufficient for the poet to hear the sound of the soul leaving the body. The puritanical idea that happiness or bliss accompanies death is flippantly repudiated by suggesting that only a fly was seen after death. The statement is paradoxical and funny. This serves as a contrast to the pain and suffering about death.

In the second stanza the poet describes the onlookers with dry looks :

> The eyes around – had wrung them dry –
> And Breaths were gathering firm
> For that last onset–when the king
> Be witnessed – in the room –

The storm of death in the first stanza is contrasted with the buzz of the fly. The presence of the fly instead of signs of immortality is significant. The narrator says she willed away her keepsakes and was approaching the magnificence of death. The fly is a sort of irritant and metaphysically used, it is a dynamic contrast with the dying. The colour of Blue and uncertain buzz suggest the final sinking of the person. The person could not see to see and this loss of control is agonising. The description is highly original and the poet reverses the conventions about the dying and the mourning. The poem questions the traditional view of death as peaceful and suggests that it is agonising and involves trauma. The pre-vision of death is presented in this poem. The windows are the perceptive sense organs which appear to fail at the time of death :

And then the windows failed – and then
I could not see to see.

This seems as a tearful complaint about death which acts like a cruel stroke of destiny and snatches away the person.

3. *I drink a liquor never brewed*

This is considered to be a parody of Emerson's *Bacchus.* In this he says:

Bring me wine, but wine which
never grew
In the belly of the grape. . .

But some critics feel that it is an early poem free from the obsessions characteristic of Dickinson's poetry. The poet celebrates the joy of living and drunk with intense feeling :

I taste a liquor never brewed
From Tankards scooped in Pearl –
Not all the Vats upon the Rhine
Yield such an alcohol :

She is inebriated by the beauty of nature. She merrily says that she has scooped all the honey of the flowers left by the butterflies. The landscape is a symbol :

When "Landlords" turn the drunken Bee
Out of the Foxglove's door –
When Butterflies – renounce their "dreams"
I shall but drunk the more !

These lines are full of echoes of Emerson's poems and the transcendental suggestions. But the poet does not accept or reject the mystical elements of his aesthetic. The poet is optimistic that she can imbibe the spirit in nature. This means that the poet can reach the over-soul in terms of Emerson's mystic. But Dickinson is pre-occupied, in this poem, with the momentary joy nature could provide and she merrily indulges in 'Debauchee of Dew'. The poem is remarkable for the alliteration and hyperbole.

4. *Because I could not stop for death*

The poet makes death a character in this poem. She visualises and personifies death in her full glory. For her death is a reliable companion, and a trustworthy mate. He in the second line of the poem refers to a person from her town, Amherst. But she was with her companion, death and so she could not oblige by stopping for him.

In the opening lines she clearly tells this in a metaphysical fashion :

> Because I could not stop for Death–
> He kindly stopped for me–
> The carriage held but just ourselves–
> And immortality.

She understands this as a last ride together. She was very polite to him. This becomes a journey to the grave. As she passes she notices her daily routine, the school, the fields of gazing grain and the setting Sun and later says that "he passed us". This shift in emphasis is a point in the poem. Her description of the house as a swelling on the ground, and other descriptions in this stanza only add to the depressed atmosphere in this poem. She recalls the Horses that carried her as if to eternity. The poem ends unconvincingly.

The poem has various levels of meaning but the surface level suggests the theme of funeral rites. The simple meaning of the poem is the procession to the grave. This has been the most repeated theme of Dickinson's poems. At deeper level, the journey could be a spiritual one. The compassionate person who would like her to take her away from death is a happy feature of the poem. But he is contrasted with Death as another and inevitable suitor to every one and there is no question of his misleading her. Death is also presented as a kind and leisured gentleman. Though it is a horror to journey to the grave the civility of death impresses her. There is no mention of suffering in this poem and this may be due to her hope for immortality.

The poem is about the imminence and inevitability of death. Life is like an unfaithful lover but death is the real, polite and trustworthy companion. This is a classical attitude to death. But she does not accept the puritanical idea of death as a means for new life or as a process of liberating the tormenting soul to reach the Divine.

Questions

1. Comment about the metaphysical aspects of the poems you have studied.
2. Write Notes on the following:
   (a) The hope for immortality and Eternity.
   (b) Death and images of death.
   (c) Fly in the poem.

3. Write an Essay on Love and Death in Dickinson's poetry.
4. Explain the significance of the poem – "After Great Pain, A Formal Feeling Comes."
5. Comment on Dickinson's style.

References

1. Douglas Duncan	:	Emily Dickinson
2. C.R. Anderson	:	E.D.'s Poetry : Stairway of Surprise
3. W. Sherwood	:	Emily Dickinson
4. Richard Chase	:	Emily Dickinson
5. Dr. S. Prakash Rao	:	A Study in Scientific Humanism.

Comparative Studies

– Compare Emily's tragic vision with that of Gray or any Poet you have studied.

III. CRITIQUE ON DICKINSON'S POETRY

Critics are divided in their opinion about the art and poetic personality of Emily Dickinson. The Academic critics have included her immediately after Poe and preceding the national poet of America namely Whitman. Though this arrangement suits a curriculum on 19th century poetry in American Litt., it is certainly not the place for her. At the same time she cannot be dubbed as a minor poetess. Most of her poems deal with love and death as central themes. Consciousness, funeral rites and graveyardism are her obsessions. A funeral procession is the recurrent image in her poetry.

The approach of Dickinson to death is ontological. She presents it as eternal silence or stillness and even as darkness. Death is a final and faithful companion. For many readers the theme of death is morbid and sickening. Poe and Dickinson evolved their aesthetic from such nauseating and morbid subject-matter. Her perception and skill endow her to use far-fetched conceits like Donne. In a poem she explicitly states:

This world is not a conclusion–
A sequel stands beyond
Invisible as music
But a positive sound

Her attitude to death is playful :

I willed my keepsakes signed away

What portion of me I could make assignable. She alludes to salvation and damnation without assuming religious tone. For her, death only intensifies senses and opens the doors for Heaven. According to some critics the thoughts of death have the purging effect on the mind.

Dickinson's love-poetry is enigmatic. Many critics have responded to her love poems as "the delusions of a spinster." She conveys love directly :

As if I asked a common alms,
And in my wondering hand
A stranger pressed a kingdom
And I bewildered stand –

These lines do not indicate any frustration but imply the erotic sensuality dormant in her. In another poem she says :

It might be easier
To fail with land in sight
Than gain my blue peninsula
To perish of delight.

Between the two matured conceptions of love and death lies Dickinson's concept of Time. She says :

They say that Time assuages;
Time never did assuage,
An actual suffering strengthens,
As sinews do, with age –

Her artistic control is evident in the lines cited above.

Having considered the most important themes in Dickinson's poetry let me turn to what critics say about her and whether we can criticise her critics. Emerson was the first one to react and called her poetry "a poetry of the portfolio". This is a half-truth. David Daiches and C.P. Snow have responded differently :

> the puritan image of a spinster concealing a body in the bedroom has become an established figure of American mythology. Her originality as a poet has never been in doubt... Witty, passionate, daringly

> metaphysical. . . some have made of her what Eliot said they made of Blake :
>
> "a wild pet for the supercultivated. . .

This is a good summing up but it does not identify her genius.

> She is described as a natural flowering of the New England tradition.
>
> She is a product of strange circumstances and art of New England.

Her vision is interpreted as contrasting modes. Douglas Duncan commented upon her outworldly uneventful existence. He says she is not at all easy to edit.

- Many of her poems are fragmentary and incomplete or doodles by which no poet deserves to be judged. This is an unfair and hasty comment.
- The secrets of her unusual art are revealed in her failures. By failure this critic means that she has not delved deep into the mystery of the erotic!
- According to Duncan the poet is a Puritan as well as a visionary.
- Richard Wilbur recognised the emotional strategy by which she could change the negatives into affirmatives.
- Duncan thinks that as an artist she found fulfilment in a celebration of suffering more than well-being, of loss more than gain, and of death more than life.
- She was a deliberate artist. Like Charlotte Bronte cultivated wild, melancholic, elevating and peculiar music. Higginson complained about lack of experience and force of experience besides Truth in Dickinson's poetry. Blackmur said that "she never knew anything about the craft of verse well enough to exemplify it." James Reeves said that "she never gave her poems a final form...she had only her judgment to consult."

Some of the oddities of Dickinson noticed are :

- departure from literary usage
- faulty grammar
- syntax is faulty
- illegitimate word-formation
- failures of metre
- false rhymes

- provincial usage
- literary archaisms
- whimsical, over-sympathetic, him–for he,
- subjunctivitis : tendency to use the subjunctive mood where indicative is normal;
- coinages : contenteder,
- provisional truths,

The justification for the host of linguistic and stylistic charges is that she creates her own technique and moulds language to the requirements of her personal voice without regard to any set conventions. In other words she was a self-conscious rebel with a direct style. Duncan hence concludes:

> ED's art was the product of a privately trained instinct.

Her poetry is desperately confessional and she did not believe in generalizations or abstractions. In this respect she is like Johnson.

Dickinson is without any pretenses of intellectualism. But she used the related skills of

- analysis;
- criticism;
- definition; and
- argument.

Besides she used many aphorisms and paradoxes. She had Romantic faith in the imagination and Puritan, classical distrust of it. Her language combines reason and strange logic.

Questions

1. Dickinson's poetry are works for mental relief and not for publication. Refute this argument.
2. The fantasy is as often Blakian as the philosophy is Emersonian, in ED's poetry. Substantiate this assertion.
3. "If poetry is to exist at all, it really must have form and Grammar and must rhyme." Do you agree with the statement of Howells with regard to ED's poetry.

4. "The noise in the pool at noon excels my piano" (Emily Dickinson). Justify her attitude to nature keeping this in mind.
5. ED is mystic akin to Emerson or the feminine Whitman – George R. Whicher. Is the statement true? Give reasons in support of your answer.
6. Self-exploitation of ED is egoism grown irresponsible in religion and decadent in morals in religion; –Allen Tate.
   Do you agree with this self-evaluation of Tate?

References

BOOKS BY THE FOLLOWING AUTHORS ARE RECOMMENDED:

1.	Thomas Wentworth Higginson	:	Emily Dickinson
2.	W.D. Howells	:	Emily Dickinson
3.	Maurice Thompson	:	Emily Dickinson
4.	Blake & Wells	:	The Recognition of ED
5.	Andrew Lang	:	Emily Dickinson
6.	Richard Chase	:	Emily Dickinson
7.	Dr. S. Prakash Rao	:	Felt Grievances

Comparative Studies

Compare the paradoxes of Dickinson with Bronte or Austin.

For Creative Writing (IGNOU)

– Make your own coinages of expression a la carte Dickinson.
– Write a conclusion for the Poem, beginning :
  Because I could not stop for Death.
– Rewrite a biographical memoir of Dickinson.

Translation

– Translate certain pieces into Telugu, Kannada or Hindi.

5. WALT WHITMAN

I. INTRODUCTION

Walter Whitman (1819–1892) belonged to a family of craftsmen. He was a printer at Brooklyn and New York and later became a journalist. He edited. *The Brooklyn Eagle* (1846 to 1848) and left it protesting about slavery and pleading for Democracy. He started experimenting with style and diction till 1855, when he published *Leaves of Grass,* which is considered a landmark of American History. This work was considered obscene and Whitman lost his job due to its authorship. William Douglas O'Connor called him "the good gray poet" and this label stuck him.

Whitman had acquired working knowledge of many things in European thought and History. Emerson and Thoreau recognised his genius and possible imperfections. He did not reason out according to any recognised system of thought and celebrated sex openly. This affected his reputation and many thought that he was preaching free sex. He was never married and there are no details about his sex behaviour. Some critics accuse him of homosexuality but there is no proof about this. He was in fact a kind and generous man. His complex personality was incomprehensible and hence the ignoramuses held contempt for him and his poetry. He was extremely unconventional, non-conformistic, and even a Bohemian in his appearance and attitudes. Whether this was a mask to his task of profession is unknown.

As a man and an artist he exhibited the following contradictions, and it is better to clear them at the outset :

- He talked about the impossibility of true love and celebrated the joy of true love.
- He denied death as a phenomenon and wrote elegies.
- He advocated a personal religion and was spiritual
- He did not believe in consistency like Emerson but was consistent Transcendentalist.

But these so-called contradictions are not contradictory or paradoxical but certain phases in the life of a complex and a pioneering poet:

First Phase	:	1855-1856
		He wrote 12 poems which formed the first edition of *The Leaves of Grass,* and *The Song of Myself,*
Second Phase	:	1859-1860
		He wrote *Calamus* poems, and poems of death.
Third Phase	:	1865–1873
		He wrote *Passage to India.*

These phases are only indicative and not necessarily tight compartments of time. As a poet he believed in the following pronouncements :

Jefferson's Declaration of Independence:

Whitman strongly believed that:

1. "in the right, the duty of men to throw off tyrannous Government and to provide new guards for their future security."
2. "it behoves everyman who values Liberty of conscience for himself, to resist invasion of it in the case of others."

These show that Whitman had a militant concern for Liberty and rebellious resistance to tyranny. In Thoreau's *Civil Disobedience* he noted:

1. "there is but little virtue in the action of masses of men."
2. "There will never be a really free or enlightened State until the State comes to recognise the individual as a higher and independent power, from which all its own power and authority are derived, and treats him accordingly."

Besides these Whitman imbibed the three basic beliefs that constituted the American tradition :

1. the Concept of Free individual;
2. the moral law based on the intellect;
3. the progress of man as self-improver.

These concepts will be discussed in due course in the contexts of the poems.

These concepts amply prove that Whitman wrote poetry inspired by the nationalistic ideals. He wanted to create a nationalist Literature with all the vitality of legends and myths of Popular Culture. Let me introduce to you some basic ideas of his longer poems which are also reflected in the poems prescribed for the study:

The Leaves of Grass (1855) is considered as product of American Transcendentalism and Romanticism. Emerson said:

> it is the most extraordinary piece of wit and wisdom that America has yet contributed.

The Whitman Cult began with this celebration, though people were quick to point out its irregular and unrhymed verses. The work was full of Oriental Transcendentalism and his contemporaries were quite unfamiliar with it. He defined it as:

> an attempt of a naive, masculine, affectionate, contemplative sensual, imperious person to cast into Literature. . .

He later asserted his poetic self and continues:

> I saw, from the time my enterprise and questionings positively shaped themselves, that the trunk and centre whence the answer was to radiate, and to which all should return from straying however far a distance, must be an identical body and soul, a personality–which personality after many considerations and ponderings, I deliberately settled should be my self-indeed. . .

This quotation must answer all the queries about his self and purpose in his poetry. His purpose was to represent an American who was "free, full and true" and hence his poetry celebrates the individual. In *Children of Adam* and *Song of Myself* he pursues the same ideal. He further attempts to fuse the individual and the cosmic nature as he perceives transcendentally and in a vision which is a reaction against Romanticism. He is a poet of the soul and a poet of the body. But he describes physical union without mentioning the theological implications of it.

In Section 48 in *Song of Myself* he presents his conception of God:

And I say to mankind, Be not curious about God,
For I who am curious about each am
not curious about God,
(No array of terms can say how much I
am at peace about God and death)
I hear and behold God in every Object,
yet, Understand God not in the least,
Nor do I understand who there can be
more wonderful than myself.

According to Whitman nature is a poem and poetry can only represent the spiritual as well as materialistic aspects of America besides the cosmic fullness of nature. This poem is called the Bible of Democracy; because he visualised development of super individuals with cosmic personalities. He wanted to fortify and encourage the citizens. He said : Produce great persons, the rest follows. He celebrated his own flesh and blood as symbols of the microcosmic nature and asserted that his fellow citizens were also the citizens of the Universe with great national pride and energy.

Whitman advocated a healthy revolt against the dead tradition in the same way as Tagore did in our country. But he was mistaken to be a morbid radical in the beginning. He was an arch-rebel of the traditions that did not inspire the citizens. He hated man-made traditions, royal formalities and priestly practices. He gave a motto that energised his times:

RESIST MUCH. OBEY LITTLE

He wanted all the outmoded social customs to be thrown out lock, stock and barrell. He realised that he was to play the role of a Prophet and he played that in full and substantial measure.

Whitman's Concept of a poet

oversimplified, it means that:

A poet must be a great and complete lover of the Universe. He identifies his subject-matter from Nature. He is a seer. He understands the Cosmic harmony, time past, present and time future. His character must represent the national character. His personality must be complete.

Function or the role of the Poet

Whitman believed that :

- a poet must perceive cosmic harmony;
- he must be the voice of Liberty;
- he must be the exemplar of quality and the fulfilment of Scientific Laws;
- he must be a realist, simple and natural;
- he must be a national.

A Perfect Poem

Whitman advocated that a poem should be :

- of perfect form,
- it is like that of a perfect animal or a tree, and it is a free specimen with organic growth,
- each part of the poem must be in proportion and harmonious with the whole design,
- A poem must tally nature.
- it should voice Democracy through freedom, heart of humanity through Love, and Soul through Religion.

The Preface to *The Leaves of Grass* states his poetics. He says:

> The American poets are to enclose old and new for America is the race of races. Of them a bard is to be commensurate with a people. . .Of all nations the U.S. with veins full of poetical stuff most need poets and will doubtless have the greatest and use them the greatest. Their Presidents shall not be their common referee so much as their poets shall. Of all mankind the great poet is the equable man.

This passage is oft-quoted and it describes the role of the poet. He says :

> (the poet) bestows on every object or quality its fit proportions, neither more nor less. He is the arbiter of the diverse and he is the key. He is the equaliser of his age and land. If peace is the routine, out of him speaks the spirit of peace. In war he is the deadly force of the war. He can make every word he speaks draw blood. Whatever stagnates in the flat of custom or obedience or legislation he never stagnates.

These lines clearly establish that Whitman was a national poet and an apostle of love and a prophet of Democracy.

Questions

1. Estimate Whitman as a poet of body and soul.
2. Whitman is a poet of optimism and pragmatism. Substantiate this argument.
3. What are the characteristics of Whitman's Poetry? Illustrate your answer.
4. Whitman was a poet of Democracy. Discuss.
5. Write Notes on :
   (a) Poet's duty is to tally nature
   (b) Transcendental aspects of poetry.
   (c) Romanticism in poetry.

References

1. F.D. Matthiessen : American Renaissance
2. J.A. Symonds : Walt Whitman : A Study
3. R.E. Spiller : The Cycle of American Litt.
4. David Daiches : Walt Whitman as an Innovator
5. Dr. Prakash Rao, S. : Encyclopaedia of Hinduism
6. Dr. Prakash Rao, S. : Milton and The Major Metaphysicals

For Comparative Studies

Compare Wordsworth and Whitman.

Creative Writing

– Translate Jefferson's piece.
– Draft a Republic Day Speech of the President.

II. WALT WHITMAN : STUDY OF HIS POETRY

1. Crossing Brooklyn Ferry

This poem was first published in 1856. In order to understand this poem and its significance Whitman's idea of creativity must be known. He says:

> Other poets celebrate great events, personages, romance, wars. . . and polish their work and come to conclusions, and satisfy the reader. This poet celebrates natural propensities in himself, and that is the way he celebrates all.

This comment is essential to understand his concept of poetry and why he wrote this poem.

In the opening lines the poet addresses the flood-tide and other aspects of nature. He says he can see them face to face. He is curious about everything including the ferry boat because hundreds ferry and across the Brooklyn river. So they are great to him in his meditations. Section I is thus a Preface to the poem. The poet gives a direct and factual account of his observation. The river brings in the associations of time past, present and future. The ferry unites all the people who have travelled by it. It is a symbol of oneness of the spirit of man. The poet recognises the identity and ferries across time. This ferry has united him and the generations to come. This identification transcends time and place and an ordinary ferry ride acquires special meaning.

The poet says :

> On the ferry-boats the hundreds
> and hundreds that cross, returning
> home are more curious to me than you
> suppose,

This is a transcendental idea of the poem. The other idea is contained in the Second section :

> The glories strung like beads on my smallest
> sights and hearings,/the walk in the
> street and passage over the river.

The setting and the principal characters of the poem are thus introduced.

In the Section II, the poet's relationship with others is indicated. The Universe is a symbol and a picture of order and not chaos.

He tells the readers :

> I am with you, you men and women of a generation,
> or ever so many generations hence,
> Just as you feel when you look on the river and
> sky so, I felt,
> Just as any of you is one of a living crowd,
> I was one of a crowd,

The river is one of gladdening aspects of nature and it unifies all humanity. The poet addresses the people in Section 3 of the poem. The images of sky, water and sunset are used to indicate the fact that:

I too had received identity by my body; the identity here refers to the spiritual identity of divine in terms of Oriental mysticism. As a poet he knows:

> It is not you alone who know
> what it is to be evil;
> I am he who know what it was to be evil:

He later describes the pleasures of the body without feeling any sense of the guilt. He confesses:

> I too knitted the old knot of contrariety,
> Blabbed, blushed, resented, lied, stole, grudged,
> Had guile, anger, lust, hot wishes I dared not speak, ...
> Lived the same life with rest, ...

These lines present a range of life and experience of the poet. The poet observes that spiritual love binds man to man and one generation to another. He says :

> I considered long and seriously of you
> before you were born.
> Who was to know what should come home to me?
> Who knows, but I am enjoying this?
> Who knows, for all the distance, but I am as
> good as looking at you now,
> for all you cannot see me.

Whitman's vision and his realization of his role are evident in the above lines. He has understood as a seer "what the study could not teach

– what the preaching could not accomplish.'' He asks the reader: ''Is it not?'' The poet's identification is total and he merges with them completely. The poem is thus a ferry of time. The poet invokes the river to :

Flow on, river! flow with the flood-tide,

The beauty of Manhattan and Brooklyn are portrayed. These lines are an appeal to the river to provide life abundantly. The river is thus an embodiment of life.

The poet realises that :

> Appearance, now or henceforth, indicate
> what you are,
> You necessary film, continue to envelop the soul,
> ...We fathom not – we love you – there is
> perfection in you also,
> You furnish your parts toward eternity,
> Great or small, you furnish your parts
> toward the soul.

The poem thus ends on a note of spirituality and divine cosmic love.

This poem is a sort of a ritual, a reverie and a poem with epic dimensions. The cosmic equality and spiritual oneness of man with the elements of nature and the Universe have been emphasized in the Vedas and Sanskrit texts in India. The poet has visualised all these dimensions with unprecedented emotional depth and aesthetic appeal. The images and utterances make the poem universal, and immortalise the poet's thoughts.

2. *When Lilacs Last in the Dooryard Bloom'D (1865)*

In the Preface of 1855, Whitman said :

> that greatest poet hardly knows pettiness or triviality. If he breathes into anything that was before thought small it dilates with the grandeur and life of the universe. He is a seer...he is individual...he is complete in himself. . .the others are as good as he, only he sees it and they do not.

This poetic principle is true of this poem; because the poet has acquired the powers and meditations of a seer : ''Ever returning spring, trinity sure to me you bring.''

This major poem is an elegy on the death of Abraham Lincoln, whom the poet celebrated as O Captain! He is not mentioned by name and in the poem we can find the vedantic and not simply spiritual acceptance of death. The evening star Venus, Lilacs and the hermit-thrush are used as symbols of resurrection and rebirth in the context of the poem. The inconsolable and permanent sorrow is suggested by the opening lines of the poem. The trinity of the poem are : the lilacs, the star and the spring. The design of the poem is as follows :

In the first section the poet mourns and later he expresses his grief. The heart shaped leaves of the lilacs symbolise love and the hermit-thrush is a bird singing the theme of death as an outlet for life. He also describes the journey of the President Lincoln's coffin from Washington against the background of mourning faces and the landscape.

The poem has a shift from section 7, when it becomes a song of sane and sacred death. It becomes an elegy for all great Americans. It symbolises their attainment of spiritual life. He also tells about the premonitions in the form of falling star indicating Lincoln's death. He says :

> The star, my departing comrade,
> holds and detains me.

and later asks himself :

> And how shall I deck my song for
> the large sweet soul that has gone?

This preoccupation forces the poet to seek spiritual solace and ultimately discover the meaning of death and the consequent lesson to the living. In the death of the great people the humanity learns a great lesson.

The poet addresses death :

> Come lovely and soothing death,
> Undulate round the world, serenly arriving
> arriving,
> . . . Passing the visions, passing the night.

This is a philosophical reconciliation to death as a means to new life. It also implies belief in re-birth. The poem moves on like a dirge and the lines mimic the movement of the coffin of Lincoln. In the mourning diverse people are united and the force that binds them is love. In this poem the growth of Love from physical to spiritual and finally to the universal level can be perceived easily. This is because he is bound with nationalism and universal love.

In the Preface he has stated that :

> the proof of a poet is that his country absorbs him
> as affectionately as he has absorbed it.

These lines are true of Whitman as he alone fulfils this poetic dictum. He has absorbed the democratic and universal love of his people and in turn he and his thoughts have been absorbed by not only of his dear Americans but by all those who empathise with his sentiments.

Questions

1. Consider Whitman as a lyric poet.
2. Describe in detail the treatment of death in "When lilacs..."
3. Is this a traditional Elegy? Give reasons and examples.
4. Evaluate Whitman as a poet of Democracy.
5. Reveal Whitman's concern for death in the poems prescribed for you and discuss how he reconciles with death.
6. Analyse the theme and structure of When Lilacs...

References

1. James Miller : Leaves of Grass
2. J.A. Symonds : Walt Whitman
3. R.E. Spiller : The Cycle of American Literature.
4. G.W. Allen : Walt Whitman.

Comparative Studies

– Compare the nationalism and universal love of Whitman with our poets such as Dinkar, H.R. Bacchan.

– Compare Whitman's lyricism with that of any popular culture celebrity.

Creative Writing and Mass Communication

– Provide an alternative ending for "When lilacs..."

– Adapt the democratic values of Whitman's Poem for a TV Special. List out the credits, scenario and effects required in the Programme Execution.

III. WALT WHITMAN : A CRITIQUE

3. *Out of the Cradle Endlessly Rocking (1859)*

This is another elegiac poem considered one of the best poems of Whitman for its theme and technique. In 1855 Preface he said that:

> The land and sea, the animals, fishes and birds, the sky of heaven and the orbs, the forests, mountains and rivers, are not small themes but folks expect of the poet to indicate more than the beauty and dignity which always attach to dumb real objects. . . they expect him to indicate the path between reality and their souls.

This principle explains as to why Whitman describes the animals to explain his mystical and transcendental observations. The poet gave different titles at different times of its publication to suggest the idea of a word out of sea. The poet reminisces, either based on real experience or so, about some death. He allegorically deals with the subject of death in this poem. The design of the poem is as follows :

Lines	1–22	:	pains and joys, introductory
	23–31	:	the nest of two birds
	32–40	:	the joy of birds
	41–51	:	the death of female bird
	52–54	:	the tragic mourning of its male
	55–70	:	the boy's reaction (the poet?)
	71–129	:	the pathos of the male bird.
	131–144	:	the pictures and images
	147–149	:	the boy's reaction to the song
	150–	:	the sea whispers : death the boy takes the clew and becomes a poet.

The theme of the poem is the education of a boy by nature to become a man and understand the mystical working of the nature. He becomes a seer and a poet to explain the sea endlessly rocking the cradle like old crone. The main tension or the conflict of the poem is the elegiac mourning of the female bird and the boy's perception of meaning and purpose of life and death in the world. His stages of illumination and transcendence are the stages of poetic apprenticeship to the nature to serve the society and unify the human soul by realising the intimations of immortality suggested by death. This is stated in the following lines:

> A man, yet by these tears a little boy again,
> Throwing myself on the sand, confronting the
> waves,
> I, chanter of pains and joys, uniter of
> her and hereafter,
> Taking all hints to use them, but swiftly
> beyond them,
> A reminiscence sing.

The sea is a symbol and representative of eternity :

> Never more shall I escape, never more the
> reverberations,
> Never more the cries of unsatisfied love be
> absent from me.
> Never again leave me to be the peaceful child I
> was before what there in the night,
> By the sea under the yellow and sagging moon,

(These lines are crucial and must be quoted by you. You must illustrate the answers with relevant lines from the texts prescribed and also the famous ones.)

The sea whispered into the boy's ear the word death and then :

> My own songs awakened from that hour,
> And with them the Key, the word up from the waves,
> The word of the sweetest song and all songs,
> That strong and delicious word which,
> creeping to my feet,
> (Or like some old crone rocking the cradle,
> swathed in sweet garments, bending aside,)
> The sea whispered me.

The poem ends on this note of confidence. Death is also rocking to and fro, which means from birth to re-birth. Whitman seems to suggest that life and death are only endless continuations. Spiritualists regard death as a new means of life. The sea is a witness to all the perennial creations of life and is hence a binding force. The cradle is a symbol of budding life and it is endlessly rocking mystically and majestically. The wet sands are a symbol of the union of the physical and the spiritual or the land and the sea of faith, in Arnoldian sense. The adult is mystically reminiscing a childhood experience and this reveals his stages of maturation as a poet.

The Critique on Whitman

Emerson made a clean break from the literary nationalists such as Cooper and Longfellow by affirming the principle of a genuine and indigenous culture. Thoreau, Whittier, Lowell, Poe, Hawthorne and Melville contributed to the affirmation or modification of this principle. By the end of 18th century Calvinism broke down and in its place Deism took place. This resulted in tendencies of Unitarianism and Transcendentalism in New England and Evangelicalism in South and South-west.

Whitman's idea of independence is radical and lies in living upto a self-discovered principle. He sympathised with Marxian socialists of his time. He was a child of the Enlightenment and the Revolution. He was nurtured by the Romantic movement. Whitman's Hero-Poet is a believer of :

- transcendentalism
- the mystery of conversion
- the trance and the sense of purification
- the salvation, the sin and rebirth.

In *Passage to India,* Whitman described the passage of the Soul from the dominant sense of physical life to the death. The same is the subject-matter of When Lilacs. . . The journey themes in his poetry are chaos to form, diversity to unity and freedom to law. He emphasized American democratic nationalism through his Hero-Poet. Whitman affirmed the Hegelian formula of progress :

– Ensemble : community
– Evolution : compromise
– Freedom : individual liberty.

Whitman provided the poetic illustration of the American idea of progress :

- The will of God whether it operates as natural law, as moral law or by direct action or intervention, must prevail in the end.
- Man as distinguished from nature is a free moral agent but his freedom is provided for by the will of God in the fundamental law that governs the Universe.

– In human affairs progress is possible only through the interaction of man's free will and previously established though not an unchangeable order.

The end pre-exists in the means. Death grows out of life, or life is implicit in death.

In 1855 Preface Whitman asserted :

> The known Universe has one complete lover and that is the greatest poet. . . He is not irresolute or suspicious lover. Nothing can jar him. . . death and fear cannot. The sea is not surer of the shore or the shore of the sea than he is of the fruition of his love and of all perfection and beauty.

These lines explain the fusion of spiritualism and sensualism in his poetry. His poetry should not be viewed as literary performance. The readers must understand the symbolism in his poetry. The following are some recurring symbols :

		Signifies
I	:	Universal aspect Soul
grass	:	green optimism, uniform hieroglyphic
loving-bedfellow	:	God
28	:	28 imperfections of human nature
sleep	:	death
ferry	:	oneness
clew	:	meaning of suffering and death
sea	:	motherhood, immortality
lilacs	:	rebirth
thrush	:	resurrection
The star	:	Lincoln

The above are some of the symbols glossed for your convenience.

Certain other exotic and subtle symbols are :

bird's song	:	death's outlet song
India	:	past of all Religions, legends
passage	:	voyage through history

ocean	:	universal meaning
botanical imagery	:	vegetation, life
bird	:	voice of nature

His symbolism is erotic, eccentric and profound. It is at times surrealistic.

Whitman was a practitioner of the aesthetics of Unanimism. Floyd Storall says that he was the product of waning Romanticism. John Addington Symonds found in his poems an expression of homosexuality of Greece. Dr. Bucke, a psychologist found cosmic consciousness in his poetry and nothing more. Howells found him realistic. The theme of universal love is derived according to some critics, from the Hindu concept of Supreme Reality and Brahman. All told, his poetry is complex but universal. He used poetry to reveal the sensations of life and death.

Questions

1. "You furnish your parts toward eternity
   Great or small, you furnish your
   parts toward the soul." – What does Whitman say in these lines?
2. The sea whispered me. Bring out the symbol of the sea in the three poems prescribed for you.
3. Analyse the treatment of love and death in Whitman's poems.
4. Whitman's transcendentalism is of a unique kind. Discuss.

References

1.	Alfred Kazin	:	On Native Grounds.
2.	Maxwell·Geismer	:	The Novel in America.
3.	Robert Spiller	:	The Cycle of American Litt.
4.	B.D. Selincourt	:	Walt Whitman
5.	Francis Murphy	:	Walt Whitman
6.	Dr. Prakash Rao, S.	:	A Study in Scientific Humanism.

Comparative Studies

Compare Whitman's symbolism with those of French symbolists.

Creative Writing for Radio and Television

1. Plan a Scenario for the Poems discussed in this collection.

2. Edit certain Poems which you think are elusive for average Indian Viewers/Listeners
3. Script a backgournd piece for a U.G.C. Telecast on this subject. Identify the list of locales and plan a shooting schedule.

Theatre Arts

Interpret certain exotic symbols of Whitman through Classical Indian Dance forms.

6. WALLACE STEVENS

Wallace Stevens was born in Reading, Pennsylvania in 1879, as a Dutchman. He grew up in farms and was a Republican. He became a lawyer in 1904 and later became an insurance man in 1916. He said

> I was the world in which I
> walked. . . what I saw came
> not but from myself.

His earliest poems appeared in 1900 in the *Harvard Advocate*. He came under the spell of Ezra Pound, and the imagist movement. Stevens was preoccupied with free verse, accurate words, bright analogies and eagerness, according to Leonard Unger.

Stevens wrote two Chinese and Japanese plays in poetic language. His New York poems were published as *Opus Posthumus*. In many respects they resemble the poems called *Harmonium*. All these poems have 'the virtue of common place.' He outlines his theory of poetry in *The Necessary Angel* (1951). Critics describe this book as :

> dense, intricate, and unsystematic, filled with contradictions; and sometimes, disconcertingly, they are full of fun.

Wallace Stevens said:

> The accuracy of accurate letters is an accuracy with respect to the structure of reality.

He has a habit of mocking either at himself or the audience. He is called an amateur of ideas. According to one scholar his poems are of two kinds :

1. the strange and imagistic
2. the lean and discursive.

Stevens is accused of being odd and underdeveloped poet. Leonard Unger says :

> there is little real development in theme or method. Analogy and interaction remain his principles.

Stevens wrote poetry waring many masks :

- the mask of manners
- the mask of dandy
- the persona of the magnifico
- the mask of the rabbi.

Sometimes the poems are considered absurd. He wrote on all matters that excited him. A poem of Stevens is considered to be a unity of the mask, the idea and the poet. He paid attention to rhythm, sound and tone. He should not be taken as a philosopher.

Stevens wrote on limited themes. He is rarely personal but he is lyrical. He has excluded the theme of Love. He thought he can write poetry on anything under the sun. Stevens said :

> The poem is its style. The style is the poet, and a
> change of style is a change of subject.

He was a realist. Like Aldous Huxley and Edit Sitwell Stevens wrote:

> Natives of poverty, children of malheur
>
> The gaiety of language is our seigneur.

Stevens always induced an element of French elegance in his poetry. He said "My dame sing for this person accurate songs." Gaiety in Poetry is a characteristic of diction." He employed :

- neologisms
- archaisms
- foreign intrusions
- "besprent words"

He rejected logical positivists and pleaded "Hierphantic phase" in poetry. According to him Americans find the British tradition inappropriate, but tolerate French tradition :

> This old, black dress
> I have been embroidering
> French flowers on it.

He used familiar terms from Baudelaire, Valery and Fargue. Critics say he imbibed from Baudelaire, Supreme fiction, nonchalance from Laforgue and the "malady of quotidian" from Paul Toulet :

> Serve the rouged fruits in early snow

They resemble a page of Toulct
Read in the ruins of a new society
Furtively, by candle and out of need.

Stevens considered that death is the mother of beauty and reality is the mother of elegance. He wrote about many such women in his poetry. He was in the French symbolist tradition. His poem "Lion in Sweden" is an example. These lions are allegorical images of bourgeois virtues. He was an imagist and admired those of Bunyan and La Fontaine. He loved analogy and used several emblems and signs to suggest something or for their own sake. Unger asks this question :

> Was he then, a Symbolist or an allegorist ?

and says the question is "unprofitable." He cites the poem "Virgin Carrying a Lantern" as a symbolic poem. Stevens gives little details, strange experiences, and a picture in his poems. In *Adagia* he says :

> A poem need not have a meaning and like most things in nature often does not have.

His poems are thus elegant though bizarre. For example :

"The Emperor of Ice Cream" produces mixed effects. This is due to use of grotesque and the quotidian meaning, the commonplace. The image of an ice cream concentrates on death and life as being part of the same. Unger says :

> The image of ice cream concentrates these meanings. At once cold and agreeable, ordinary and festive, it is a symbol of life and death. Imperative mood and the finality of the final rhyme add as much to this strange composition as the commonplace details : last months' newspapers in the first stanza and, in the second, the dresser lacking three glass knobs, the horny feet.

The above passage is a good example of the approach to Stevens and hence the long quote. The lines he has in mind are :

Call the roller of big cigars,
The muscular one, and bid him whip
In kitchen cups concupiscent curds

The poet is producing the effect of the opposites in the emperor and the ice cream :

Let the wenches dawdle in such dress
As they are used to wear, and let the boys
Bring flowers in the last month's newspapers,
Let be finale of seem
The only emperor is the emperor of ice cream.

"Peter Quince" is an elegant poem. His elegantiae are suave and malign. The relations between the inner and the outer, the observer and object are the subject-matter of the poem.

Stevens is an extremely absorbing and a real poet without any pretenses. His poems are enjoyable. He uses bright and clear images. He considered poetry as supreme fiction. Yeats and Dylan Thomas appreciated his poetry. He used the technique of Painting in poetry. He put on the masks of a Lecturer, a rabbi and so on.

Questions

1. Write a critical appreciation of the poem "Emperor Ice Cream".
2. Stevens believed in interaction and dialectical opposition. Discuss.
3. Consider Stevens as a poet of 19th century.

References

1. Leonard Unger : Wallace Stevens
2. Frank Kermode : Wallace Stevens
3. R.P. Blackmur : The Double Agent
4. Harriet Monroe : A Poet's Life.
5. Allen Tate : Sixty American Poets.
6. Dr. Prakash Rao, S. : Felt Grievances.

Comparative Studies

Compare the images of 'Ice Cream" with any known poet you have in mind.

Creative Writing for TV

Write an Episode script, frame by frame, for "The Emperor of Ice Cream."

7. NATHANIEL HAWTHORNE

I. THE SCARLET LETTER

Nathaniel Hawthorne (1804-1864) belonged to the family of magistrates of Salem, Massachusetts. He believed that his family ancestry was cursed because of their strict and rigorous punishments to people, particularly the quaker women. He makes it a point to refer to bitter prosecution by his ancestors in his novels. About this he says in *The Custom House* :

> John too inherited the persecuting spirit, and made himself so conspicuous in the martyrdom of the witches, that their blood may fairly be said to have left a stain upon him. . . I know not whether these ancestors of mine bethought themselves to repent, and ask pardon of Heaven for their cruelties; or whether they are now groaning under the heavy consequences of them, in another state of being.

This is considered as a bitter trial of ancestors and he also confesses :

> At all events, I, the present writer, as their representative, hereby take shame upon myself for their sakes, and pray that any curse incurred by them may be now and henceforth removed.

The above sense of sin and guilt haunted him throughout his life. As a teenager he developed the 'cursed habit of solitude'. He further developed the idea :

> I do not want to be a doctor and live by men's disease nor a minister to live by their sins, nor a lawyer and live by their quarrels. So, I do not see that there is anything left for me but to be an author.

Hawthorne was completely aware of salem history and the lives of the Puritan colonists. His life and times conditioned him :

- to have a Puritanical attitude to Sin and suffering

- to be introspective
- to turn to moral allegory
- to be confessional, symbolic and desperately secretive.

Soon after marriage in 1842, he stayed at Concord, near Boston and was intimate with Emerson and Thoreau. He did not, however, approve of their radical brand of transcendentalism. He later took to service as Surveyor at Salem, and enriched its life.

After a good deal of creative writing, he wrote in 1850 *The Scarlet Letter*. It is regarded as one of the great classics of American fiction.* He was a friend of Herman Melville and developed a symbiotic relationship with him. Melville was influenced by Hawthorne and he emulated him. He dedicated *Moby Dick* (1851) to Hawthorne. By now *The Custom House*, *The Blithedale Romance* were also popular. He wrote a Campaign Biography of *The Life of Franklin Pierce*, idealising the President of U.S. As a traditional reward of literary sinecure he was awarded Consulship of Liverpool in 1853. He lived in England from 1853 to 1857. These years occupy the descriptions of *English Note Books*.

The following aspects of Hawthorne need attention :

- his craftsmanship : architectonic or unity of structure
- sense of style : poetic prose
- deep moral nature and humanistic insight
- Puritan tradition and belief in Original Sin
- skilful use of allegory and symbolism
- Pathos in place of sentimentality
- Gothic elements : mystery and terror

THE SACRLET LETTER : TEXTUAL STUDY

Introduction

In his note book Hawthorne entered :

> the life of a woman, who, by an old colony law, was condemned to wear the letter "A" sewed on her garment, in token of her having committed adultery.

This work is a good study of Gothic Romanticism and also has some elements of historical nature coupled with the sentimental novel. Freudian approach or Psychological criticism to this novel would reveal that it is a

*It is an all time classic and a favourite ingredient of Senior Cambridge curriculum of Elective English Litt. – Dr. SPR

fascinating study of repression. Historically, it is a record of 17th century New England. Moral approach is the popular subject of the critics as the theme deals with sin and its consequences.

The Plot :

The plot of this novel is neatly organised and hence critics praise the architectonic quality of the novel.

Chapter I : *The Prison door*

The novelist makes a grim beginning by refering to a Prisonhouse and a cemetery. A rose-bush under the sainted Anne Hutchinson is mentioned. The author announces that this is a tale of human fraility and sorrow.

Chapter II : *The Market Place*

Before a 17th century Boston Prison people await Hester Prynne, a female prisoner, guilty of misconduct. She comes out with a girl of three months old, with a letter "A" embroidered on her bodice. The misfortune and disgrace of her are described. Her past fills her mind as she stands on the scaffolding under the pillory. This is a flashback of her sin.

Chapter III : *Recognition*

She recognises her husband in the crowd. She was considered an antinomian (one who believes that Christian morality is not binding on him/her) or a Quaker (a sect) Adultery was regarded as 'the deepest sin in the most sacred quality of human life.) This man was Roger Chillingworth. Another man called John Wilson was the clergyman of Boston condemns her sin and announces that Rev. Dimmesdale would find out her partner.

Chapter IV : Hester and her baby are unwell and nervous. Hence, the jailer fetches a physician, who is her husband and a revenger Roger Chillingworth, a deformed old man. He was her husband and hence he wants to know the name of her lover.

Chapter V : *Hester at her need*

Released from the prison, Hester lives in a cottage in the out-skirts. She was a skilled knitter.

Chapter VI : *Pearl*

Pearl is the daughter and product of a guilty passion of Hester. She had the native grace and beauty. She was not in favour of any discipline, and was impish.

Chapter VII : *The Governor's Hall*

Hester goes to Governor Bellingham's bungalow to deliver gloves. She learns the plan of citizens to separate Pearl from Hester on religious grounds. She was regarded as a scarlet letter in human form.

Chapter VIII : *The Elf and the Minister*

Roger has established good reputation as physician and a friend of Dimmesdale. Wilson asked Pearl whether she is a Christian or a fairy. Her answer surprises everybody and Hester tells the Governor that the child is her life. The child was regarded as a punishment and a reminder of her sin.

Chapter IX : *The Leech*

The doctor is believed to be an agent of the Serpent. He lives with the minister with some secret hope.

Chapter X : *The Leech and His Patient*

The minister has animal nature in him. He does not suspect the doctor's desire to spy on him. There is a discussion about people dying without confessing secrets. They see Pearl and her mother and Roger comments that there is an impish tinge in her.

Questions

1. Identify the influences on Hawthorne and how they have shaped the plot of *The Scarlet Letter* ?
2. Give the synopsis of the Plot of the novel and comment about its merits.
3. Write a note on the Puritanism in the novel.

References

1. F.O. Matthiessen : American Renaissance.
2. Robert E. Spiller : The Cycle of American Litt.
3. Dr. Prakash Rao, S. : "Current Issues in American Litt.".

Comparative Studies

- Compare Hawthorne's concept of Sin and retribution with any puritanical Indian author.

Translation

Attempt a translation of Chapter VI and Chapter X in your language.

For TV/Theatre

1. Write a screenplay adapting this novel for Indian or Satelite TV.
2. Mention some probable actors and locations for filming this novel. Suggest a couple of Indian variants of Title for Bollywood, Tollywood.

II. NATHANIEL HAWTHORNE : TEXTUAL STUDY OF *THE SCARLET LETTER*

The plot-development in the ten chapters suggests that Hawthorne is a master of psychological action. The emphasis in the novel has been to probe the inner most regions of consciousness.

Chapter XI : *The Interior of a Heart*

Roger Chillingworth nurses a deep malice in his heart. He wants to blackmail his victim. Dimmesdale was popular as a miracle of holiness. But he was guilty and was always tormented by the thought of shame. He fasted and sought penance for his mistakes. He thought of a new plan of self-torture and set out of his home on a night.

Chapter XII : *The Minister's Vigil*

Dimmesdale stood on the scaffolding and experienced thoughts of remorse. He cried wildly so that his mistake is recognised by the town. Those who noticed him did not realise what he was doing. But this chapter is revelatory and puritanical in the treatment of the subject-matter. He experiences a vision of Hester and Pearl reaching the scaffold. He lost his glove which was found by the sexton. A letter was found on the sky that night.

Chapter XIII : *Another View Of Hester*

Hester meets Dimmesdale accidentally during the night. Seven years have passed after her first ignominy and she felt pity for him. She consoled herself as a Sister of Mercy. People gave the meaning for the letter ''A'' as able, angel etc. She became reflective after her meeting with him. She meets Roger one day along with Pearl.

Chapter XIV : *Hester and the Physician*

Hester calls on the old physician who teases her in a strange manner. She found in him a fierce and fiendish look on his face. She requests him not to torment Dimmesdale, the priest.

They argue vehemently. The minister had nightmarish experiences everynight and he welcomed death. The doctor was happy that he is taking revenge on the minister.

Chapter XV : *Hester and Pearl*

Roger's vindictive and malicious nature makes Hester hate him. She recalls the time she had spent with him as his wife. Pearl asks her mother as to what the scarlet letter means, and why the minister kept his hand on his heart.

Chapter XVI : *A Forest Walk*

Pearl asks her mother to tell the story of a Black man who carried a book with him. Hester notes the minister walking along the forest track. This chapter is full of symbolism.

Chapter XVII : *Pastor and His Parishioner*

Hester calls out the minister who is nervously despondent. They question each other about their physical existence as both regarded each other as spirits. They exchange their despair and miserable condition. Ruined souls do not find peace. Hester tells everything about Roger, and how he had violated the sanctity of heart and its consecration.

Chapter XVIII : *The Flood of Sunshine*

Hester's suggestion that the minister should leave Boston gives hope and joy to him. He notes that Hester has greatly endured the suffering and has gained the native strength. He resolves to flee with Hester whom he now feels indispensable. He has regained his capacity for joy. Hester removes the scarlet letter from her bosom. When this stigma was lost she felt a great relief. She removed her cap and exhibited her beautiful hair. She called her Pearl and she came to her mother.

Chapter XIX : *The Child at the Brookside*

Hester introduces Dimmesdale and Pearl to each other, and draws attention of the similarities of their features. He felt that the brook was separating the two and that the child was estranged from him. Pearl asks her mother to restore the scarlet letter and she obliges her. When the minister blesses Pearl by kissing on the forehead she washes her forehead in the brook.

Chapter XX : *The Minister in a Maze*

Dimmesdale and Hester plan to quit Boston. Mistress Hibbins, the witchlady meets him. He speaks hypocritically with her and the doctor.

Chapter XXI : *The New England Holiday*

A holiday was declared to instal the new Governor. Pearl and Hester wait at the market place to see the procession of the Governor. She sees Roger smile dreadfully at her.

Chapter XXII : *The Procession*

Hester awaits to have a glance of the priest. She recalls her sad and passionate talk with him in the forest. Hibbins asks Hester whether the minister had met her in the forest. Dimmesdale began his Election sermon in serious tone. Pearl is asked to convey the message of a shipmaster. She told her mother that Roger too would accompany them on the ship.

Chapter XXIII : *The Revelation*

The minister came to the scaffold and held the hand of Pearl and spoke to the gathering. He uncovered his chest and fell on the scaffold. Pearl's tears fell on her father's cheeks, and he died. This is a stirring and pathetic climax of the novel.

Chapter XXIV : *Conclusion*

Most of the people saw the scarlet letter "A" imprinted on his chest. Several people thought differently about this. Many felt that the minister fell in the lap of Hester to suggest that in the eyes of God all are sinners. Roger too died, after an year. He bequeathed his property to Pearl, the demon-child or elf-offspring. Later Pearl was married to an aristocrat. Hester was a source of strength to many in distress. When she died she was buried close to the grave of Arthur Dimmesdale. The letter "A" was put on the tombstone and this became a legend.

The writer ambiguously and religiously portrays the Puritan sentiments in this chapter. He gives psychological insights to situations and actions.

The Theme of Sin, Crime and Punishment

The following are some of the approaches to *The Scarlet Letter* :

- as a story of Sin and suffering
- as a psychological novel
- as an archetypal tragedy of a woman
- as a Puritanical novel
- as a study of guilt romance.

All the above approaches revolve round the following aspects and the central basic concept is the Seventeenth century attitude to Sin and retribution in general and adultery in particular. The Eighteenth century concept of a Gentleman is to a great extent a reaction towards this critical theological debate. The aspects that require intensive study are:

- Is Hester guilty?
- Is it proper to disregard Pearl?
- Is the punishment meted out to Roger adequate?
- Irony and symbolism of the novel
- adultery and Christian concept.

These aspects will be dealt with in detail.

The first aspect that deserves prime consideration about the novel is the sense of guilt and Sin. The implications of these are portrayed in the lives of Hester, Roger and Dimmesdale. The reactions of the general public is also communicated through the crowd and scaffold scenes in the novel. The erosion of personality and deterioration of self are admirably portrayed in the novel. What a person thinks sinful is not a personal but social affair. Hawthorne represents the host of feelings through subtle, Christological symbols.

Nature in this novel is symbolic of 'Wilderness of error' and other symbols are :

Symbol		*Meaning* (in the words of Hawthorne)
Pearl	:	"freedom of a broken law"
prison	:	black flower of society
nature	:	a force contrary to moral law
rose-bush	:	moral blossom
baby in arms	:	image of sinless maternity
infant	:	redeemer of the sinful world
A	:	adultery
fire	:	God's judgment : purificatory
needle	:	passion
embroidered clothes	:	freedom of speculation
Black Man	:	Devil

brook in the forest	:	(1) a carrier of sorrows, (2) boundary between two worlds, (3) symbol of estrangement.
forest	:	moral confusion, place of adultery, innocence, romantic individualism
the scaffold	:	punishment, death, sin, confession.

These symbols and the author's own words that indirectly suggest their meaning are glossed for your easy comprehension. The general substance of the novel is lost sight of by the contemporary readers who are used to the same theme in the films as well as the media stories.

The idea that Sin and guilt pervert and destroy human happiness and personality is central to Puritan interpretation of the novel. In many respects it is a sermon and an emphatic plea to be away from the seven deadly sins. The conflicts in the minds of Hester and Dimmesdale is because of this idea. The act of committing the sin is destiny and the consequent loss of innocence and human element is predestined. They are incapable of faith and the society regards them as demon-offsprings and they are condemned.

Another ingenious interpretation of the novel employs the doctrine of *felix culpa* : Fortunate Fall. Sin is considered to be a source of wisdom. Because of their moral turpitude and fall, Hester and Dimmesdale are compensated by self-realisation which is hard to acquire. They are also constant reminders of do's and dont's of the society. They are the mocking presences of listening to the devil's dictates.

This novel has attracted the attention of romantics who feel that it is not a sin to respond to one's natural urges. According to them it is wrong to punish such aggressive expressions of individualism. Hester and Dimmesdale have committed adultery owing to natural urges. They go another step further and argue that it is the society that has sinned against nature. Hester according to these existentialists is heroic and a feminist who earns the distinction of a Sister of Mercy by her acts of humanity. Hester is defying the code laid by Puritans because she is passionately in line with Dimmesdale. The writer creates sympathy for Hester and Pearl and this gives rise to ambiguity or different interpretations of various situations in the novel.

That Mrs. Hawthorne wept and complained of grievous headache, that Thackeray felt pathetic speaks of the 'triumphant success' prior to its publication in 1849. Henry James considered this novel "beautiful, admirable and extraordinary". Hawthorne was a great contemporary influence on Poe. Both the writers specialise to portray the dark and gothic aspects of human soul. The inner life of the characters who are like people matters most to Poe and Hawthorne.

Questions

1. Discuss *The Scarlet Letter* as a story of sin and punishment.
2. Comment on Hawthorne's concept of Sin in the *Scarlet Letter*.
3. Consider the *Scarlet Letter* as a study of the impact of Sin on the human soul.
4. Explain the significance of the scaffold scene in relation to the theme and structure of the novel.
5. Compare and contrast the attitudes of various characters to the sin in the novel.
6. Write Notes on the following :
   (1) The problem of evil in the novel.
   (2) The tongue of flame.
   (3) Hawthorne as a rebellious Puritan.
   (4) Romance in the novel and the novel as a romance.

Points for Discussion

1. The faults of *The Scarlet Letter* are a want of reality and an abuse of the fanciful element – Henry James.
2. *The Scarlet Letter* is a romance and not a novel... Hawthorne
3. A man like Dimmesdale should not commit a crime like adultery... Thackeray.
4. It is one of the great love stories of the world – Mark Van Doren
5. The scaffold is the beginning, Chapter XII the middle and Chapter XXIII is the conclusion of the novel.

References

1. Mark Van Doren : N. Hawthorne
2. F.O. Matthiessen : American Renaissance
3. Henry James : The Life of Hawthorne

4. Robert Spiller : The Cycle of American Litt.
5. Terence Martin : N. Hawthorne
6. Dr. Prakash Rao, S. : Current Trends in ELT (For discussion on Hawthorne's teachability for ICSE students).

Comparative Studies

Compare certain aspects of Poe's fiction with those of Hawthorne.

Media Studies on Popular Culture

Are contemporary Horror Works and films extensions of Gothic Fiction ? Explore.

Theatre Arts

Write a Soliloquy of Hester or Dimmesdale.

Creative Writing

Eaborate chapter XXIV into many chapters keeping the following points in mind :

1. Pearl marrys an aristocraf
2. Hester turns helpful
3. the legend of Pearl.

8. HERMAN MELVILLE : *BILLY BUDD SAILOR*

TEXTUAL STUDY

Melville (1819-1891) is a prominent American author and his name is synonymous with *Moby Dick* with epic features portraying the idiosyncracies and pride of a budgeoning nation. He was born and brought up in New York and he understood the urban culture very well. Till 13 years of his age he experienced penury and poverty with its attendant calamities. He did odd jobs as a clerk, book-keeper and then as a teacher. He nurtured a romantic idea about sea and life on it.

The sea fascinated him. He went on a whaling ship during 1841-1845 to the south seas and learnt everything like an undergraduate. He even made certain adventures to an island and he was made a captive by the aborigines of the island believed to be full of cannibals. All these strange experiences gave him an insight into life and times universal to man. He had similar experiences at Tahiti and he was rescued by the U.S. Navy and repatriated.

Melville made a fantastic decision to settle down to full time creative writing, soon after his marriage. *Typee & Omoo* were published and he was a success commercially and literally. Heavy symbolism and allegory marred the reputation and sale of *Mardi*. Only the success of *White Jacket* and *Redburn* could revive him professionally as an entertaining writer. These novels are not so well known in India and only *Moby Dick* receives the need of academic attention in Seminars and allied discussions.

By this time Melville was getting the recognition and he was compared with Whitman. The reasons were the New York background, and the Civil War. They were born in the same year and died in 1890s. Melville's proximity to the then celebrity, namely, Hawthorne, gave a new break to his fictional career. Some literary historians credit Hawthorne for the allegory and epic scope of *Moby Dick*. If it is so, Whitman added the epic dimension to American Poetry.

These achievements are no doubt at the World-level or international level. Poe and Hawthorne enlarged the biographical and literary interest on Melville. Emerson and Thoreau did the same for Whitman. *Moby Dick* was dedicated to Hawthorne. Commenting about this, Wager says :

> About *Moby Dick* there is a kind of inscrutability and universality in the possible interpretation of the symbols that is comparable to that of the most Powerful writing of both West and East – Shakespearean, Homeric, Biblical, Far Eastern.

This is a true estimate of Melville and what made him and his writing famous is :

> White Whale, which has so aroused Captain Ahab that he assembled a crew from the four corners of the earth, infected them with his monomania, and led them to their destruction..

The implications of all this are :

" – the self-destructive nature of personal vengeance,
– the excessive demands of Puritanism
– the dangers of perfectionism."

These are comparable with those of Hawthorne's ideals, exemplified by his characters. Ahab is comparable with Taji and both share the symmetry of fear about life and society. The spirit of Hawthorne's *Blithe dale Romance* is to be found in Melville's *Pierre* (1852).

Billy Budd, was written a few years before his death and it was published posthumously in 1924. It has a dramatic quality and a touch of historic reality. The scene of the novel is set in 1797, the aftermath of French Revolution. The mutiny ridden British Navy and a sailor form the touching scenes of this novel. Billy is innocent but he is hanged. Billy's soul is blessed and sailors sing his glory and innocence.

The significant work of Melville is *Moby Dick* (1851). The story of Captain Ahab and his hunt for the white whale which mutilated one of his limbs is the main story of this novel. He is attacked by the whale and the ship sinks. Only the narrator, Ishmael is saved. The pursuit and revenge motif became central to 19th and later 20th century fiction. Hemingway borrowed the following aspects in re-telling the story of Ishmaeal as Santiago :

– poetic language
– symbolism
– evocative and simple descriptions.

At the time of writing of *Billy Budd*, Melville's personal philosophy was that of a nihilist if not a stark nihilism of Hemingway. He cultivated according to some of his friends the attitude of rejection or self-denial. Written in 1891, this work received attention as a novella. According to some critics he was mentally deranged or even insane at the time of writing this work. It does not in any way diminish its value as true art and a magnum opus of Melville.

The Theme of *Billy Budd*

The central concern in this novel is man's ability to seek peace and harmony with society at one level and with God at another level. Melville's early novels reject the need of society for man. They also reject God's role in making man happy. This nihilism pervades this work also. His protagonists are self-reliant and question the mystery and obscurity of God. However, it is difficult to diagnose this attitude as atheistic and as agnostic quality because Hawthorne would have condemned such testament of rejection. In many respects they are rebel-victims of testament of acceptance.

Melville pursued this with vigour in this novel. Evil, violence and Mental agony are called the 'darker aspects of human nature' and he probes them with his life-time maturity and offers a true picture of what he perceives. The villainous officer Claggart plans to take revenge on Billy Budd. He is jealous of his happiness.He plots against him accusing him of mutiny on the ship. Billy loses self-control and strikes him resulting in his death. The dilemma of the Captain becomes morally terse because he is fully aware of the elements of their nature. Captain Vere upholds the law though the innocent person becomes a victim and the benefit of doubt is not passed on to him. At a moral level Billy is innocent whereas legally he must be punished. The ideas of order and social welfare are put to trial in the contexts of the novel. In the final analysis, this novel is a study of nature of justice. The 19th century ideas of justice were that the good of the society must prevail, even if it means that the principles of natural justice are not probed into. It also points out that justice in the practical sense of the term is imperfect and not universally valid. Billy is thus crucified or made a Christ-like figure. Santiago is another version of him. His hanging is full of Biblical imagery. W.H. Auden agreed to accept Billy as Adam if not as Christ.

Psychologically Billy's effeminate and his gay looks excite a homosexual and pervert, Claggart. This is revealed in the incident, of spilling of the soup. He expresses this repressed feeling as hatred and death-wish for his 'mate'. Billy is normal. He says :

God Bless Captain Vere.

There is little choice between social order and social anarchy, according to Melville.

Symbolism in *Billy Budd*

The elaborate symbolism of this novel could be summarised as follows :

Billy	represents	goodness, youthfulness
Vere	,,	laws, virtue
Claggart	,,	devil, disharmony

The names of ships have allegorical parallels and elements of myth are suggested by them.

- colour imagery is highly suggestive
- biblical imagery : ascension, fleece, Lamb of God etc.

Questions

1. Comment on Melville's characterization with special reference to Billy Budd.
2. Compare the Puritanical stances of Melville and Hawthorne.
3. Describe the part played by Claggart in the novel.
4. Comment on the theme and technique of the novel.
5. Analyse various types of imagery and symbolism in the novel. Are they integral part of the narrative ?

Points for Discussion

1. *Billy Budd* is a work of true art. Evaluate.
2. Billy is a Christ-like figure. Elaborate
3. The digressions in the novel are important to the central issue. Substantiate.
4. The testament of acceptance theory is defended by this novel. Refute this statement.

References

1.	Richard Chase	:	H. Melville : A Critical Study
2.	Leon Howard	:	H. Melville
3.	Harry Levin	:	The Power of Blackness : –Hawthorne, Melville & Poe
4.	Lewis Mumford	:	H. Melville

Creative Writing

- Identify suitable cast for the Dramatis Personae of this work.
- Retell the story of *Billy Budd* in the rhetoric of Hemingway.
- Write a dramatc Poem on Ahab or Billy.

9. MARK TWAIN : *THE ADVENTURES OF HUCKLEBERRY FINN*

Mark Twain (1835-1910) was born in Florida, Missouri. During 1848-69 he worked as a printer, reporter and even as a steam boat pilot. In 1869 he met William Dean Howells and published *The Innocents Abroad.* His romance with Olivia Langdon of New York culminated in their marriage in 1870. In 1876 he published *The Adventures of Tom Sawyer* and in 1885 he published this novel of epic dimensions.

His real name was Samuel Langhorne Clemens. He lost his father at the tender age of 12 years. After struggling he became a steam boat pilot and the river left an indelible imprint on his imagination. He wrote several novels, anecdotes, speculations, recollections, diatribes and later an Autobiography. His reputation as a novelist is now established and he is estimated as novelist of the order of Dickens and Dostoevski. He is looked upon as :

- a symbol of American Dream
- an accepted artist of the unliterary public
- a symbol of moral concern
- a narrative voice and an embodiment of the typical American Character.
- the New England writers called "Brahmins" considered him as a humorist.

These are all half-truths and only a detailed study of the novel will reveal his quest for underlying truths.

TEXTUAL STUDY

Chapter I : This Chapter links with *The Adventure of Tom Sawyer.* Tom and Huck discover the money hidden in the cave by the robbers. Huck is an orphan and he is adopted by the widow Douglas. The money is invested and the boys are given a dollar a day. For Huck who lived with the slum ruffians the new life is hard. He meets Tom at midnight.

Mark Twain establishes the point of view and the life of ante-bellum world and its language. The use of dialect reinforces authenticity in the novel.

Chapter II : Tom and Huck trick a Negro slave Jim and go to the cave in the woods. Tom announces his plan to form a gang of robbers so that all could become rich. They discuss how to ransom the prisoners.

Chapter III : Huck is badly dressed and Miss Watson scolds him. She asks him to pray. Huck's father is believed to be drowned, due to heavy drink and falling into the river. Tom and the gang plan to rob and kill but they are met with a gang of school children.

Chapter IV : Huck goes to school and learns to read and write. He does not like his father and like others he is superstitious.

Chapter V : Pap who is fifty year old does not accept the civility of Huck. He demands money from Huck which he refuses. The judge and the widow go to court to take Huck away from Pap.

This chapter reveals the view of Huck that Pap and Douglases exist in every society and one cannot possibly reform this situation.

Chapter VI : Pap tries to recover the money of Huck through the court. He beats and extorts money from him. He takes Huck and confines him in a log cabin on the bank of the river Mississipi. In a drunken condition one day Pap criticizes the Government, for giving freedom to Negroes and tries to stab Huck. Huck escapes and protects himself with a gun.

Chapter VII : Huck returns to the cabin with five fishes. Pap goes to the town to sell the logs of wood which they have found in the river. Huck creates a mock-suicide and spills the blood of a pig on his clothes. He travels to Jackson Island in a Canoe.

Chapter VIII : Huck notices Pap, Judge Thatcher, Tom Aunt Polly and others searching for his dead body. They superstitiously float bread and quicksilver in the river. Huck builds shelter for himself in the woods. He meets Jim, the Negro slave of the widow. Jim thinks that Huck is by now a ghost and begs not to hurt him. Jim reveals a secret that the widow wanted to sell him to someone, Orleans and so he ran away. The beliefs and culture of people in the frontier are described in this chapter. Their natural wisdom and superstitions are mentioned.

Chapter IX : Huck and Jim live in a cavern in the woods. One day they find a frame house floating with a gashly dead body in it. . . Jim plays the role of a father to Huck and both regard each other as human beings. Leslie Fiedler's Freudian analysis on this comradeship is that it amounts to homosexual relationship. The absence of women in the island and Huck's search for his father force them into a union.

Chapter X : Huck is more curious about the dead man, and Jim superstitiously wards off any discussion on it. They rob the dead man of certain possessions and find eight dollars in his pockets. Jim is bitten by a snake believed to be the mate of a rattlesnake that Huck killed for fun. He nurses him for many days. Jim suggests that Huck should go to town in the disguise of a girl and find out about things. He trains Huck.

Chapter XI : Huck goes in disguise as a girl and knocks a

house on the outskirts. He gives out his name as Sarah Williams and invents a story about him. She tells him about the murder of Huck and the suspects are Pap or Jim. Huck goes to the island, wakes up Jim, and sails into the river in a boat.

Judith Loftas is a character who symbolises the hospitality of frontier people. Huck has matured and developed humanity. He quests for freedom and this chapter reveals that humanitarianism ultimately triumphs over racialism or a narrow consideration.

Chapter XII : Huck and Jim journey for several days and nights. When they reach St. Louis on the fifth night, there is a storm and they see a steam boat which has collided against a rock. Huck sees two murderers in it. The focus in this chapter is on horror and violence. The fury of the frontier is unleashed here.

Chapter XIII : Huck and Jim are marooned. He sympathises the scoundrels and arranges for their rescue. There is a conflict in his inner-self and his conscience.

Chapter XIV : Jim and Huck find many things in the wreck. They take cigars and go into the woods. Huck reads stories about kings and others from the books they have gathered from the wreck. They discuss Solomon's story. This chapter is full of comic fun. Huck thinks : "You can't learn a nigger to argue." The white man superstitiously believed in his racial superiority.

Chapter XV : They reach near Cairo. This chapter informs us about the intimacy and emotional dependence of Huck and Jim about each other, Huck has made a common cause with Jim and deliberately he plays mischief with Jim without any reason.

Chapter XVI	:	Jim feels feverish to feel free. There is a conflict in the mind of Huck. He is also afraid of people who are looking for run away niggers. When some people want to check the raft, Huck pulls a fast one, and says that his father is in and that he is suffering from small pox. They float forty dollars on a log towards Huck and go away. Jim thanks Huck for saving his life. After a few days, they jump into the waters of Ohio. This chapter describes ''positive assertion made through the painful triumph of Huck's sympathy for Jim''.
Chapter XVII	:	Huck is chased by barking dogs. Some people think that he is not an intruder and they welcome him. Huck forgets Jim for a while. Huck calls himself as George Jackson and becomes a friend of Buck.
Chapter XVIII	:	The hosts are enemies of Shepherdsons. The feud arose because of some land dispute. Huck fetches the Bible that Sophia forgot in the church. There is a slip and indication of time on it. Buck is shot dead by some horsemen. The raft is a symbol of hope in this novel. Civilization is not encouraging and it is full of violence and horror, according to Twain. The genteel tradition and their brutal shootings are narrated in an absorbing manner.
Chapter XIX	:	The journey downstream, probably, has no purpose in the novel. Huck and Jim appreciate the peace and the beauty of the river. They meet two people and plan ''double-team together''. They are in fact tricksters and impostors. In those days, some people posed as kings and Dukes to cheat gullible passengers and it was part of the frontier life.
Chapter XX	:	The King and the Duke enact some scenes from Shakespeare's *Richard II* and *Romeo*

and Juliet. The writer portrays the mob behaviour and their sentimentality. Puritanism and confessions are attacked indirectly in this chapter. The world outside the raft is considered evil. The raft is a symbol again of purity and innocence.

Chapter XXI to Chapter XXIII	:	The tricksters continue their acts of entertainment and cheating. Colonel attacks the humanity. Huck observes that the spectators are prepared to throw rotten eggs. Jim regrets about his slapping of his deaf and dumb daughter. This chapter contrasts the values and experiences of different types of people. Huck is revealed as a boy of conventional values.
Chapter XXIV to Chapter XXVI	:	The double-team decide to sail for some distant place so that they could dupe the villagers. They meet a stranger and enquire about the details of the village. They dupe the Wilks girls of six thousand dollars. Joanna questions Huck about his life in London and asks him to swear on the Bible. Huck does not like to cheat orphans. He has some ethics and does not like the victimization of human beings. His sense of right and wrong is now developed in him.
Chapter XXVII to Chapter XXX	:	Huck steals the money kept in a coffin and it is buried. The frauds make false promises to girls to take them to England. Their Negroes are auctioned. Mary Jane sobs for the sale of slaves. Two new comers, namely, Harvey and William arrive and assert that they can prove who they are. They go to the graveyard and open the coffin only to find the dollars. Huck and Jim run straight into the river. The impostors quarrel and only obey the law of the jungle.
Chapter XXXI to Chapter XXXVIII	:	The frauds continue their vocation of cheating the villagers. They continue missionying,

doctoring and mesmerizing and telling fortunes. Huck writes a letter to Miss Watson informing her about the place where Jim is. After chapter XXXI Huck assumes the name of Tom Sawyer. The tone and the mood of the novel also change. This has been criticised by many critics, but defended by Eliot and Trilling. On the Phelps farm he is rescued by a Negress from the dogs. Huck meets Tom. Tom mistakes Huck for a ghost. Later the frauds are punished and Huck feels sorry for them. He protests cruelty in any form and even in matters of punishment.

Tom and Huck try to find Jim. He is imprisoned at the back of the farm. They see Jim chained to a cot. In this Chapter XXXV, Twain's distrust of romantic novels could be seen, particularly those of Scott and Dumas. They influenced Tom to such an extent that he likes to follow those adventures. Twain seems to feel that books of romantic adventures would spoil the adolescent imagination. Tom's style in these chapters is comic. They take a rope ladder and create absurd situations.

Chapter XXXIX to Chapter XLIII : Tom and Huck decide to carry out their plan of putting rats, rattle snakes and spiders into Jim's cabin. They trouble Aunt Sally and Uncle Silas. They write anonymous letters. Finally they rescue Jim. Tom is hurt by a bullet. The doctor treats him, and praises Jim for nursing Tom. Old Watson was dead and she has set Jim free in her will. Tom acts as Sid and Huck plays Tom so far. Aunt Polly's arrival is *deus ex machina* and provides safe ending to the novel.

In the last chapter, Jim is set free and rewarded. Tom gets well and Huck is happy that his adventure is over. As a boy of 14 the narrator-actor tells things realistically and narrate his experiences. The authenticity of the novel is thus enhanced.

The Novel as an Epic

The novel is described as a comic epic of American in Prose. The epic struggle of Huck lies in his search for the sense of belonging and being. His life values and experiences are described in detail in the course of the novel. It is a long narrative, serious and propounds moral truth. The central figure, Huck is a noble and a virtuous figure.

Huck symbolises archetypal Americans and their aspirations and values. The struggle of Huck is in fact the struggle of America becoming a nation. The weaknesses of the people are exposed. It is comic and is narrated with lot of irony and satire.

The Structure of Huck Finn

This is a puzzling question about the structure of the novel. Some regard it as great art and some consider it technically defective. Eliot considered it as a great novel. It has diverse settings and situations and the final unity of the novel is elusive. Hence, some consider it as an artistic failure. In the novel, the river also becomes a character and a unifying device. It does not have a single unifying principle. The backbone of the novel is the river and the novel has been contrasted with great epics. It is a social satire on slavery and hypocrisy. It is a realistic novel.

Twain's Humour

He is a great humorist basing his style on absurdity and hyperbole. It releases the emotional tension in the novel. It is multidimensional in range and character. You must recall all the incidents in the novel to substantiate these statements.

Questions

1. Discuss the role played by Jim in the novel.
2. Trace Huck's spiritual growth in the novel.
3. Critically appreciate the theme and technique of the novel.
4. Discuss the novel as an epic of America.
5. Recall the role of the river in the novel.

Points for Discussion

1. Huck seems the first Existential hero, the improbable ancestor of Camus's Stranger or the protagonists of Sartre, or the negative characters of Hemingway.

   – *Leslie Fiedler*

2. The values for which formal Christianity stands are in the end seem to be the opposites of the virtues professed by the pious.

   – *Daniel Hoffmann*

3. Huck takes them as Acts of God which pass away, and yet one side of this stoicism is an attitude towards time in which the immediate present is accepted as the immediate present.

   – *W.H. Auden*

4. It moved Rudyard Kipling to discover another sagacious boy beneath a cannon and conduct him down an endless road. Discuss.

References

1.	James Cox	:	Mark Twain
2.	Carl Doren	:	The American Novel.
3.	Leslie Fiedler	:	Love and Death in the American Novel
4.	Dr. S. Prakash Rao	:	Modern American Fiction (CIEFL)
5.	Harry Levin	:	The Power of Darkness
6.	Spiller &c.	:	The Literary History of U.S.

Creative Writing for IGNOU Students

– Compare certain aspects of Twain with Dickens or Dostoevsky.

– Write a screenplay adapting the work to Indian TV.

– Write a note on :

1. Films that employ comedy in the graveyard.
2. Literary Values in Contemporary Film Scenes/Songs.

10. RECENT THEORIES ON AMERICAN LITERATURE*

—Dr. S. Prakash Rao

The paper identifies main recognizable trend-setting theories on American Literature and discusses their significance. A theory, whether in Science or Litt., serves as a means of organising the current perceptions and possible conjectures that lie between the unknown and known. They generate considerable curiosity and contribute to the coherence of a discipline. Facts and explanations have to be organised into a conceptual order. I.A. Richard's *Principles of Literary Criticism* (1924) warned critics of ''the chaos of critical theories''. The questions relevant at this stage are: Does litt. contain theory? Does criticism inevitably contain theoretical component? Can there be a true theory of litt ? The critical debates of earlier decades were monistic and believed that theory is *ignis fatuus*, irrelevant or unnecessary.

The theories of literature and approaches discussed in this paper are:

- Realism, Naturalism and Novel of manners.
- Fiction of ideas
- Fiction of forms
- Fiction of existence
- Fiction of essence
- Formal and Structuralists theories
- Marxist, Marxian theories
- Archetypal approach
- Freudian theories
- Behaviouristic theories
- Cybernetic theory, entropy, and technological prophecying.

Though by no means the above theories are conclusive about the nature of experimental litt., in America they constitute the all-embracing major landmarks and lines of communication between the creative minority and the mass civilization under scrutiny. Sub-theories and

---

*A modified essay by me rendered in Creative Writer's Workshop held at IGNOU HQ and in the All India Conference at Osmania University.

concepts that have informed various sub-genres have been comprehensively dealt with in the course of this discourse.

Sociologists have identified alienation as a major symptom of Western society and its literature. Daniel Bell in *The End of Ideology* (1962) pointed out that many intellectuals and writers have nurtured themselves on a 'Cult of Alienation'. This theory, along with anti-intellectualism popularised the notion that Capitalism creates among writers with radical social values, a tension. Irwing Howe, Norman Mailer and Wright Mills are illustrious examples to this hypothesis. The sociological imagination was characterized by traditional and scientific points of view. Some writers share the unified world view which Eliot found in Dante's culture. This makes recent American litt., a "psychological gyroscope". It voices the aspirations of a society which has moved from production to consumption and from work to leisure. Much of the recent fiction like that of Pynchon's and Ludlum's is like a radar screen and the like of it is not discernible in Eurocentric or Afrocentric litt., David Riesman's *The Lonely Crowd* (1950) has inspired recent writers who create autonomous, privileged persons and are "inner-directed".

The conflicting visions of Self and Society and the discontents of contemporary civilization is seen in writers who have subscribed to the Behaviouristic theory. Behaviourism believes that demonstrable and measurable responses to stimuli lie in man's actions. Psychoanalysis, on the contrary believes that man's actions must be understood by knowing his personal history and through introspection. Many SF writers and other mainstream writers such as Barth and Vonnegut have created Psi-Fi. Skinner's *Beyond Freedom and Dignity* (1971) recognised the freedom and litt. of dignity. Anti-utopian and futopian fiction emerged in SF like Huxley's *Brave New World* and Orwell's 1984.

The identity conferred upon a self based upon Erikson's identity stated that "the capacity of the ego to sustain sameness and continuity in the face of changing rate," is the true identity. American Jewish fiction and Metafiction confirm to these trends and approaches.

Technological prophesying and Frankenstein complex also characterized recent litt. The feeling created by fiction is that the unimaginable seems real. Mumford viewed technology as a product of human culture. This view is largely reflected in War litt. McLunan's view is that a medium is not only a device of communication but a structuring of the senses and the mind. Personal and social effects of media is pursued by Pynchon and Heller.

The post-Einsteinian world of Cybernetics or the information theory challenged the traditional Judeo-Christian idea of God as the creator. Mailer and Pynchon made use of these themes. The theme of Entropy has become a dominant issue in contemporary litt. Metafiction and Religious SF are the most conspicuous responses to the thermodynamic quest of man's world. This state of religious thought changed the vision of America as "God's country". Paul Tillich represented Neo-orthodoxy combining protestantism with modernism. He did not ensure obedience to a moral code but stressed a situational ethic assimilating. Marxism and Existentialism based on tragic sense of life.

Let us examine these theories in various sub-genres of American literature using the parameters of the theories and approaches so far outlined. Contemporary writing includes various themes and orientations involving radical experimentation and expression. Literary criticism has been an exercise in consensus to divergent inquiry. Formalistic criticism has given way to the archetypal criticism.

In promoting a personal vision of the world modern novelists ensure considerable enterprise and communicational impresarios. Those who are guided by the theory of Realism and Naturalism pursue the sensibilities of Joyce, Proust and Woolf in the use of narrative resources. But in order to follow a distinctive tradition evolved by Theodore Dreiser, Sinclair Lewis and Edith Wharton. Realistic novel in recent years depicts the inscrutability of historical forces and the interplay of individual action. The theme of American Civil War popular in 1950s is no longer popular in fiction and non-fiction. Cold War paranoia abounds in the fiction of Hiller, Mailer and their followers. These terms are not necessarily to be applied to novelists of inter-war period. Realism and Naturalism would continue to have their pride of place as novelists influenced by the Marxist or Existential ideology also tend use these concepts. This is true of the Jewish, southern, black or feminist fictions which give the complete vision of America and voice social despair and individual initiative. Heller continues to write initially like Dos Passos and Hemingway in the spirit of a war journalist. Asimov is indebted to Zola, Tolstoy for aesthetic materialism in *The Caves of Steel* and *Gods Themselves*. Naturalism in Steinbeck is revealed in his fascination of Biology and nature. Hemingway's heritage can be discerned in the works of James Jones, Nelson Algren, Mailer and Gore Vidal.

Realism of recent American fiction is marked by the shadows of political events, social movements and fate. Naturalism emphasizing heredity and environment and humanity's elemental nature influenced the fictional theories of 1970s. James Jone's first work *From Here to Eternity* (1951) powerfully depicts army life in the war of Pearl Harbour. Its hero cannot "understand nor explain nor change" like any other type of naturalistic protagonists. Gore Vidal's fiction *Myron* published in 1974 is a historical war novel. Though the plot is weak, the range of his art and craft are extensive. His historical novels are iconoclastic and researched. Vidal also reveals to me stray influences of Deconstructionist theory. His historical novels are a dialectic of the contemporary self. Mailer's recent writings recall his earlier works: *The Deer Park* (1955) and *An American Dream* (1965) particularly *Why are We in Vietnam* (1967). His concern for applying recent, vigorous narrative techniques employing SF notions of a disc jockey rivet our attention to the Metahistorical aspects These recent trends and techniques and the use of non-fictional resources have made some critics to dub him as a journalistic writer. Mailer's conception of reality and transcendence, which have not been adequately probed display an "Apocalyptic vision" and firm grappling with the elements of Litt. Mailer described his novels as 'non-fiction novels' of the proper genre. His ideological contention though less profound than Barth, Heller and Pynchon, they have an unprecedented vitality. They dramatise a historical moment and Mailer's rhetoric is in conjunction with the trends and developments in the progressively dynamic genre.

It is believed that Naturalism, and the novel of manners are "the enduring mountains in American fiction". Ethnicity appears to be the epicenter of fiction in the works of Joyce Carol Oates' *Wonderland* (1971) and *Do with Me What You Will* (1975). John Cheever's *Falconer* (1977) deals with the incarceration of Prof. Ezekiel Farragut for the murder of his brother. Its technique lies in a series of monologues of guards and visitors to Falconer prison. Its psychological profoundity and metaphoric celebrations of human spirit are its fine points as works of fiction. J.D. Salinger established a reputation equal to that of Hemingway through *The Catcher in the Rye* (1951) and *Seymour* (1963). The deepswell of regionalism in recent writers is attributed to the growing popularity of ethnicity in all the sub-genres of American Litt.

On the post-war Southern fiction Faulkner introduced the system of a cycle of novels set in a make-believe county called Yoknapatawpha, Warren and Welty also employ the dialectical view of history. Flannery O'Conor, Walker Percy and John William Corrington illustrated in their stories theories of self. Is the self the Soul? Is the cryptic question asked by them. O'Cohnnor declared in "The Nature and Aim of Fiction" the view that the artist must "intrude upon the timeless, and that is only done by the violence of a single-minded respect for the truth".

Recent writers though less known in India, are Reynold and Cormac McCarthy. Reynold's *A Generous Man* (1966) mentions :

"What I have chronicled is my own world. . . that world which has seemed to me. . . to exist *beneath* the world perceived by other people, that world which seems to impinge upon, to colour, the shape of the daily world we innerit." McCarthy's *Child of God* (1973) depicts survival problems in a southern country. It is a sort of grotesque pastoral. Another character Lester Ballard portrays necrophiles in the manner of Poe. Usher and Ballard are psychopathologically lonely. Southern novel in all these cases adheres closely to modern historicism and it is said that "the southern novelists' imagination of the self's condition waits upon further revelations of the congruence of self and history". The southerner's ethnicity tackles the core problems of existence in the fictional world portrayed by them.

Before the contribution of other distinguished writers of the nascent genres is reviewed, mention may be made about new and radical theories in Socio-cultural Linguistics. Ferdinand de Saussure's (1857-1913) revolutionary ideas about the language as a sign-system with its own logic quite independent of the reality it is supposed to represent, affected the new wave of writers. Structuralism believes that "through language, a culture maps out a reality according to its own requirements, defining just what the individual will be able to say, think and perceive. . . . and each maps out different one". Claude Levi-Strauss's anthropological explorations on primitive cultures brought `untraditional results'. Ronald Bartnes' study of fashion, sport, TV, food and so on, Jacques Lacan's psychoanalytical study of Saussure's work, Michel Foucalt's research on madness, sanity, crime, normality and deviancy have affected the bearings of Literature. An individual's mind is perceived as a 'Social Construct' defined by its language and culture pondering upon Eternal Truth and expressing it as a poem or novel. A work in light of all the pronouncements made, can transcend its time and place. As a refreshing contrast, Marxists consider capitalism as the root of all evil and everything else. They might perceive in Keats' Odes rising industrialism. Marxists have gained the missing link between social organisation through language and society. Louis Althusser argued that 'ideology is more than a set of ideas. He says that 'ideology saturates our lives, right through to the unconscious level and our sense of self'.

Freudian Semiotic and anti-semitic theories and their pet notions can be discerned in the contemporary Jewish Litt. It exhibits urban, liberal, progressive dynamism compared with other genres. Some scholars credit it with the balancing of conservative and agrarian bias of the Southern Litt. It is committed on one hand to the East European *Shtetl*. Theories of Non-acculturation distinctly colour the mood of the Jewish American literature. Nazi holocaust is built into the structure of its litt. Saul Bellow (1915), Bernard Malamud (b. 1914) and Philip Roth (b. 1933) dominate this sub-genre. Bellow has referred them as the Hart, Schaffner and Marx of American literature. Bellow's dangling hero Joseph dangles between civilian and military status during World War II. *The Dean's December* (1932) like *Herzog* adopts dialectic theory. Bellow feels that non-acculturation is an inevitable condition of human existence. Bernard Malamud makes the dangling man an outsider and an alien in the ethnic neighbourhood. The archetypal framework of *The Fixer* (1960) and *Dubin's Lives* (1979) bring Yiddish cadences and moral visions. Philip Roth, who is influenced by less theorizing of Jewish tradition concentrates on naturalistic theories in *Letting Go* (1962) and *Portnoy's Complaint* (1969). Freudianism and anti-semitic theories influence the humour, style and hyperbole of Roth's fiction.

Social history and Psychology get the better off than Jewish acculturation in the poetic novels of E.L. Doctorow (b. 1931). *The Book of Daniel* (1971) an account of spies and *Ragtime* (1975) a fragmentary anthology on Americana, reveal political theories of the Seventies. The novels of I.B. Singer *Shosna* (1978) and *Enemies : A Love Story* (1972) depict the New York lives of Jews who escaped the Holocaust. These novelists reveal influences of historical and literary Yiddish with tinges of East European imagination. Joseph Yiddish with tinges of East European imagination. Joseph Heller's *Catch-22* (1961) is a bitter attack on the institution of war and a parody on Pentagon. Though it was reviewed in a hostile and pejorative manner at the time of its release the world is right now in a better position to accept it after "the operation desert storm". The vitality of the Jewish American novel lies in its universal appeal compared with the Israeli Fiction with its Talmudic and Yiddish orientations. The socialistic and psychological realism has made this genre a much-talked-about and commented about in American Litt.

As one scholar remarked, "Jewish novels sound a note of alienation from the mainstream culture, black novels constitute a symphony on the subject''. Ralph Ellison's *Invisible Man* (1952) is yet to be challenged in terms of theory, theme and technique. A young blackman's disillusionment with American Capitalism and later with Socialism finally leading to the discovery or invisible black identity has been portrayed with coherence to the cyclical view of history. Many of the apologists of Black American Litt., canvass for it a distinctness which can be found in James Baldwin's *The Devil Finds Work* (1976).

In the field of Experimental fiction and deconstructionist fiction feminists have found new ideas helpful to project a new literary identity. French reminists like Julia Kristeva, Luce Irigaray and Helen Cixons revised the views of Jacques Lacans on Freud. They produced a new ''non-phallocentric'' theory of psychoanalysis which has not met with adequate success.

Constant experimentation has brought to Structuralism a state of permanent revolution. Radical criticism of Jacques Derida altered the sausserean notions of Sixties that behind every text there is an authoritative 'speaking voice' that can 'tell' us things. Derida felt that words can only refer to other words and texts to other texts. This has brought to criticism the element of intertextuality. Post-structuralist and Deconstruction theories emphasized ways and rhetorical tricks employed by writers to convey truth. Some call these theories as skepticism with a mixture of Marxist theory. Derida felt that there is no such thing as free thought.

Harold Bloom heralded the Reader-Response criticism. He denounced his deconstructionist colleagues of Yale School as nihilists in his *The Anxiety of Influence* (1975) the viewed history of literature as one of oedipal struggle, each new generation of writers trying to dissect it with 'creative misreadings'. Some Germans like Hans Robert Jauss and Wolfgang Iser propounded 'Husserlian Phenomenology'. In America Stanley Fish argued that readers themselves construct the texts they read.

The major trend and exciting litt. in the recent decades is a surrealistic and fabulistic writing. The theories of European Absurdists and the Gothicists and Beats are found composed in this sub-genre. Some have called Metafiction a body of fiction about the making of fictions. This recent theory considers plot, character, setting and theme as the true enemies of the novel. John Barth calls for an unfamiliar thinking about fiction and creates ''the litt. of exhaustion'' while some talk about the need for the list of replenishment. Raymond Federman calls it ''Surfiction'' drawing the notion of the surrealists that life itself is a fiction. Robert

Scholes prefers the term "Fabulation" for the theories on fabulistic didacticism. William Gass, calls the new wave as 'metafiction'. Popular metafictionists are Barth, Pynchon and Donald Barthelme and Kurt Vohnegut Jr. whose work requires several hours for explication and analysis.

Recent trends and theories in American fiction are in fact a series of thoughtfully contemplated, unconventional fictions. Several concepts from religion, myth, science, history, mathematics and political thought are combined with fantasies to drive home the narrator's point of view. W.H. Gass has said that "many of the so-called anti-novels are really metafictions". John Barth states explicitly that "we tend to think of experiments as cold exercises in technique. My feeling about technique in art is that it has about the same value as technique in love-making". Hence, contemporary experimental fiction resorts to new modes of perception and fictional forms. Fictional theory according to Robert Scholes, is based upon the assumption that :

- both the conditions of being and the order of fiction partake of a duality which distinguishes existence from essence.
- the order of fiction somehow reflects the conditions of being which make man what he is.

Accordingly, much of the current fiction is "fiction of Ideas". This is animated by essential ideas as in mythic fiction as found in folktales. Fiction or Litt. springs from human desires and deeds. "Fiction of forms" usually imitates other fiction. It accepts the legacy and repeats it. Existential and behaviouristic theories energise the "fiction of existence" which imitates the forms of human behaviour and not the forms of fiction. It represents reality and hence it is mimetic". The "fiction of essence" is concerned with the deep structure of being as the fiction of behaviour is concerned with its surface structure.

The formal and structuralistic theories explain how fiction is created and how it works. Behavirourists are concerned with what fiction means. Lukacs and Leavis applied theories of social consciousness to behaviouristic theories. All these western notions have viewed society as evolving in time toward a better life for men and American Litt., is expected to contribute to that evolution.

American fiction has received the need of attention it deserves as an articulate medium of contemporary angst. This does not mean that

American drama is less important but generally it is held that it is less avantgarde and intellectual by its very nature. The moorings of American drama lie in its cross-cultural validity. Recent theories have brought in the dramatic devices as in Lorraine Hansberry's *A Raisin in the Sun* (1959), Arthur Miller's *Death of a Salesman* (1949), musical *Do Re Mi* (1960) by Jule Styne. O'Neill's reputation is phenomenal and is based on symbolism and naturalism of his well-known plays. He applies linear and circular notions in *Journey* and *Oedipus Rex*. Tennessee Williams represented total American sensibility. Miller and Williams used fatalist theories opining that an individual has no choice. Miller is pre-occupied with post-Freudian notions about original sin in his plays of 1972. William Inge and Robert Anderson experimented with drama but with little success. Many playwrights moved from television to stage. The new generation of Edward Albee produced professionals as he said in the Preface to *The American Dream* that it is an "attack on the substitution of artificial for real values in our society". Other Broadway hits include Ribman, Martin Duberman and Israel Horovitz. The trend in the Seventies is the evolution of two genres namely farce and musical comedy. Keeping pace with life the play became lavish, earnest and expensive though less imaginative. John Cander and Fred Ebb developed satirical voices reviving the musicals.

Recent trends in American poetry follow the maxim of Ezra Pound that the poets are the antennae of the race. The disjunctions of contemporary life was voiced by Eliot's *The Waste Land* (1922) and Pound's *Cantos* (1925). This was an attempt at cultural seismography. Eliot it can safely be generalised adhered to the doctrines to suggest the futility and anarchy of modern, urban civilization. Great language experiments and individual stylism marked the innovations of Robert Frost.

Emersonism and rugged individualism of Thoreau were the firm basis of recent poetry. Several trends were set by Auden, Edmund Wilson, Pound, Ransom and Tate. Classicism and Romanticism equally influenced the poets on one hand and on the other the formalism of Yeats, Frost, Stevens and Auden. Tate believed that poetry is public discourse and it involved rational organisation.

Another trend was set by Robert Lowell who effected a change from grandiloquent poetic style to colloquial idiom. Despair in the tradition of Keats was used by Berryman who also used the dream song stanza. It is believed that his personal emotions were in fact the emotional climate of modern age.

Anne Sexton, Sylvia Plath and W.D. Snodgrass, revolutionised the style of Lowell and Berryman. They represented a school of dissidence and they were influenced by the New Criticism, Uninhibited self-exposure. Sylvia Plath, encouraged by her husband Ted Hugnes, wrote personal, confessional and even hallucinatory poems which were also culturally symbolic. The subject, range and tone underwent a sea change. James Merrill continued the autobiographical strain and verse-making.

Among the native Americans Scott Momaday turned out fine poetry and novels. James Wright, Mark Strand used projective theories of Poetry. Surrealistic poets using satirical, absurdist and detached modes of writing were created by the New York School of poets. Mention also must be made of Frank O' Hara for his reflective and sensory poetry. The trend of expressing one's own experiences in an aesthetic manner has undergone sea-change in contemporary America.

Creative Writing and Theatre Arts

1. This piece is an experiment in Literary theory and Literary history. Attempt Similar pithy essays on :
   - Recent Trends in Creative Writing in India
   - Recent Trends in Theatre
   - Recent Trends in Experimental drama
2. – Recent Trends in Documentaries
   - Recent Trends in Game-Show on TV
   - Recent Trends in Literary Criticism.
3. Recent Developments in Mass Communication

   Recent Developments in Marketing and Advertising

   Recent Developments in Bussiness Communication.
4. Identify themes and techniques not so far depicted on TV or Films.
5. What are the archetypal characters/situations exploited by the Art cinema and commercial cinema in
   - the portrayal of anti-heroes.
   - the portrayal of non-heroes.
   - the portrayal of antagonists.
   - the portrayal of lady characters.

11. CURRENT ISSUES IN MODERN AMERICAN FICTION

– *Dr. S. Prakash Rao*

The present monograph is a study (1984-87) of issues of theological, aesthetic and cultural value that abound in the genre of modern American Fiction. It is a critical inquiry into representative works of archetypal modern American fiction considered chiefly in terms of Apocalypticism and with regards to current issues that energize the genre. It is indisputable that in an age like the present one marked by social and religious ruins men of faith, intellectuals and artists seem subject to a sense of cosmic destiny as exemplified by biblical under-currents such as 'Pisgah Vision' and 'Ezekiel's Vision' which are indeed apocalyptic in that they abound in factual futurological revelations. Based on a Judeo-Christian Apocalyptic Design a Scale of reference philosophically and theologically this study attempts to identify, interpret and analyse the basic current catalytic issues in Religion and Aesthetics which influence man's understanding of self and society–Issues which are germane to Apocalyptic Vision that seeks to embody the portents awaiting man and prognosis of his imagination. Such a study has not been attempted so far since the issues have not received the need of critical attention nor have they been considered apocalyptically and from inter-disciplinary approach. This is an attempt also to motive *Rasika gana sabha* for a kind of *rasotpatti* which is not easily obtainable in the study of any other art form.

Modern American Fiction has become a genre formed out of realignments of expectations of die-hard intellectual milieu. It records contexts of extraordinary experiences of sensitive and often misunderstood as 'eccentric' people. It does not present a homogeneous pattern but divergent patterns and vehicles of thought. In this sense this genre is the greatest expression of really-real modern life. The crux of modern fiction seems to be its pronounced subjectivity, the assertion of self and robust pessimism reinforced by tragic-irony of life that characterizes the aesthetic experiences of the novelist. The novelist's vision of life and the spirit that shapes his materials and the prognostications are of vital and aesthetic interest.

Post-war American novelists such as Norman Mailer, John Barth, Thomas Pynchon, Philip Roth, Bernard Malamud, to name a few, have been dubbed as "absurdist" or "revolutionary" on the basis of their vision of life or Zeit geist. Works of science fictionists such as Isaac Asimov, Robert Silverberg (for a full discussion q.v. my book ICAS 813.45 A831 R21 ASRC, Hyderabad) offer the prognosis and social diagnosis of futuristic societies, futopias and dystopias. The overall configuration of modern obsessions, social and psychic problems are fictionally represented. A multiform vision of the end of the world and a deep expansion of a doomsday mentality of modern culture has been stylized as apocalyptic vision. Apocalypse combines the Miltonic aspect: would to God that all Lord's people were prophets" and Blakean aspect : "I must create a system or be enslaved by another man's perspectives." The branch of study that pursues these multiple visions is Apocalyptics.

Apocalypticism reinforces the function of literature as a record of cultural seismographs. The socio-cultural convulsions and cataclysms of human societies, their sense of well-being constitutes apocalyptic elements. Apocalyptic concepts defy conventional metaphysic, contemporary poetics on the so-called "Linguistic policing" or categorization. Apocalyptists are essentially theological and apocalyptic literature alludes to visions, biblical world-view, the doctrine of the icons, pessimism and eschatological expectations. It revitalizes the mythological doctrines that serve as foundational concepts of fictionists. My doctoral dissertation entitled "Apocalyptic vision in Modern American fiction 7.8.85" (ICAS 813.5409 P. 89 ASRC 442 PP) traced the origins of the concept of apocalypse. The concept has been identified as "the child of prophecy, yet diverse from prophecy" as proto-apocalypse arising out of Hellenistic-oriental syncretism. The Greek verb Kalupsis means to uncover. Milton used the term to denote any revelation and Swift employed it to report any sensational disclosure. The concept underlines the fact that the real cause of evil is godlessness and evil forebodes catastrophe. The imminent apocalypse envisions as a punitive measure an end of sinful humanity. Several types of apocalypses have been described. History records the notion of Isaianic apocalypse in 6th Century B.C. central to apocalypticism is the Book of Revelation of St. John of Patmos and provides the basis of other texts such as Book of Daniel. The role of core religious concepts and their influence upon contemporary culture have been substantially discussed in the thesis.

Modern American apocalyptic fiction has positive, dynamic perceptive ability or future-consciousness. Lucretius viewed apocalypse as crisis of faith. Bacon viewed it as an anticipation of nature and how science imposes skepticism whereas religion imposes empire of faith over sense. Descarte and Comte believed that supernatural means are indispensable elements of apocalypse. Darwin termed it as a mystery of mysteries. Freud attributed it to psychic activity and treats it as hysterical paranoia. It is my firm belief that Darwinian and Freudian views are reductionist views and they ignore the theological impulse of man. Apocalyptic visions are not inspired by diverse speculative and meditative moods and euphoria of fear or emotional psychosis but also of transcendental selves.

For the purpose of research a Judeo-Christian apocalyptic design has been outlined, by me sociologically, which are indicative of mythic and mythopoeic conditions of reality:

- the pre-catastrophe world
- the stage of the destruction of ideal or society
- catastrophe motifs: flood, fire, locusts, plague, atomic war
- the beast with the number 666
- loss of faith
- Armageddon motif
- Christ's appearance, renewal
- Rejuvenation of a new world order.

Earlier studies have been scant and the above orientation is missing. These stages closely correspond to the stages of sinful exhausted humanity, emotional psychosis, sense of despair, sense of doom, crisis of belief and disbelief, apocalyptic hope and finally the triumph of good over evil.

In my doctoral dissertation I argued, rather convincingly as some academics remarked, that modern consciousness, in reality was propelled by apocalyptic impulse which characteristic or living principle is genetically endowed. Such a hypothesis was established based on Darwinian principles, Huxleyan perspectives, Russell's deductive axims and above all Frye's views on Biblical typology. Apocalyptic despair constituting a sense of doom and a crisis of belief and disbelief enforces a vision which is not merely an extension of the mental-spiritual agonies of Chaucer's pilgrims and tragic-ironic visions of Eliot's *The Waste Land* as certain critics hasten to conclude. Apocalyptic fiction, unlike the average run-of-the-mill fictive visions, embodies apocalyptic hope comprising of the triumph of good over evil (which theme was glorified by sixteenth century literatures) resurrection, renewal and rejuvenation of the old systems. The new world order hopefully resembles the kingdom of God – a dream vision Jewish literature celebrates even in current times. Lack of hope is attributable to a demythologized paranoid doomsday feeling. This factor is identified by science fictionist David Ketterer as apocalyptic imagination. This investigation has proved that the concept is sustainable, viable, reliable and valid in all the twelve representative novels held to scrutiny and textual analysis.

The central thrust and purport of earlier study is the axim that apocalyptic has been an obsessive and dominant contemporary form in modern literatures: European, American and the Commonwealth. This is not due to international fallacies or super imposition of the findings on American fiction on other genres. Further exploration of the concept reveals that it does not lend itself to a set pattern or configuration and presents multiple levels of reality such as the Joycean aspect of History being a nightmare, Wellsian aspect of fiction's service as cultural diagnosis and conscience-keeper of a generation. Hardy anticipated this factor in *Jude*, as man's effort to seek harmony in 'chaos of principles'. Bernard Malamud's and Doctorow's radical Jewish humanism testify this fact.

The twelve novels abstracted here reflect distinctive visions. Their novelists create idiosyncratic myths to mime the reflection of reality. They have been spiritual followers of classical apocalypse or the Judeo-Christian view of apocalypse. Their novelists concur, as demonstrated, on the issues outlined below.

- apocalypse is an essential aspect of reality and supra-modern sensibility.
- apocalypse captures the mood of time and in its vision of disaster has hope.
- apocalyptic mode of fictive narration is suitable to the novelists of recent times, in other words, the novelist has to be a political historian to justify his art and craft.
- art as a principle of ordering reality cannot compete with life on equal terms and hence non-fiction methods or metafiction (Barth) or Transfiction (Mailer) are to be used in place of conventional techniques.
- man's search for utopia or dystopia are analogous to the conceptions of Heaven and Hell respectively and that this process would continue.

– man's powers either aided by science or technology are finite and man's choice in any catastrophe is limited within the frame of Free will and Predestination.

– Post-Cataclysmic sensibility requires that scientific humanism be promoted.

Dream of Annhilation: Anatomy and Morphology of Apocalypticism

The Visions of novels abstracted below seek a regenerated universe. They point out psychopathological syndromes. Their vision is a cultural expression of current milieu and the result of present race-experience. Apocalyptic despair becomes a unifying central metaphor. Man's condition as Hemingway's *The Sun Also Rises* and Faulkner's *The Sound and the Fury* is typified by the phrase 'Ants on the burning log'! As the fictionists of the "lost generation", the melancholy of the two world wars and their woes were reminiscent of Biblical apocalypse. Hemingway depicts a vision of war-wearied effigies who have lost their sense of beauty and sense of duty. Faulkner's novels typify modern society as a wasteland. Faulkner's man has become a prisoner of society. On similar terms, Hemingway's matador represents pro-toapocalyptic force held in check and the symbol of the crucifiction stands for remedial rebelvictim. Hemingway and Faulkner, from this insight, depict the apocalyptic cycle of death, of abnegation of self-darkness or chaws which crystallize as a unique vision. Spanish civil war and the Depression which serve as a backdrop to their novels reinforces their apocalyptic vision. In the sound and the fury Yoknapatawpha country is the ideal society awaiting catastrophe chiefly at emotional and personal level. In the pre-apocalyptic stage, doom is linked to error of sin as typified in the incident of Caddy's loss of virginity. The vision of agony points to the condition of loss of traditional values, aimlessness and fragmentation. Hemingway and Faulkner porway existential visions and voice the pangs of unassimilable nightmare, anguish and dilemmas of life, Brett tells jake in The Sun.

It makes one feel rather good deciding not to be a bitch, "It's sort of what we have instead of God." This reveals the total wreckage of life experienced in twentieth century life, indeed, the greatest disaster for life has become, living. Briefly outlined, the current issues anticipated by Hemingway and Faulkner are: (1) Break-up of established institutions, (2) Sense of despair, (3) Nihilism, (4) Crists of belief and disbelief, (5) Search for identity, (6) Apocalyptic inner conflict: chaos of principles, Moral confusion, (7) Demythologization, (8) Intentionally prophetic allegories of reality, nightmare, (9) Confrontation with the alien within,

(10) Gloomy mental life : solipsism, Paranoia, hallucination and guilt, (11) Godlessness, (12) Insecurity, (13) Inauthenticity, (14) Doomsday feeling.

The above topics can be studied profitably by those who offer American Litt.

(Extension Lecture to M.A. Final by Editor, Dr. S. Prakash Rao)

Further Study

1. Identify current issues in commerical cinematography or cultural studies.
2. Argue the case for Indological interpretations of Western classics that are derivatives of Indian cultural ethos.
3. Enumerate the ideas that have trafficated between the East and the West.

References at ASRC : ICAS

1. Dr. S. Prakash Rao 813.45 A 831 R21

2. Dr. S. Prakash Rao 813.5409

12. SAUL BELLOW : *MR. SAMMLER'S PLANET*

Saul Bellow is regarded as one of the most prolific and intellectual novelists of America. Several monographs of his writings and critical studies have appeared in recent years. India's contribution to Bellow studies is rich, though it is not fully acknowledged. The characteristics of his characters, their tensions, peculiar predicaments described in the novels have aroused considerable interests dangling in the minds of his admirers. The interest is growing and his place in modern American fiction seems assured. He is an anti-apocalyptic writer and his character Herzog in a letter to Vinoba writes:

> I'd like to join your movement.
> I've always wanted very much to
> lead a moral, useful, and active life.
> I never knew where to begin.

Such a yearning for peace, coherence and understanding of one's situation was hardly articulated by modern novelists in such eloquent and simple terms as Bellow had done.

Bellow's fictional method and the choice of themes appeal to Indian mind with a distinct *samskaras* termed at times Hindu or even Indian. But its essential quality is Jewish though he has called the jewish tag "false and wrong" in his interviews. He does plead the Jewish case, which he and his researchers stoutly deny. These things you may do well to remember and analyse them:

- conspicuous ethnicity.
- rootlessness.
- assertion of traditional Jewish stances.
- personal, complex, involved arguments about issues.

Jewishness is a fact of his existence and however secularised one pretends to be it remains. But he is not an orthodox Jew.

The Adventures of Augie March, Henderson, The Rain King and *Herzog* were received with great admiration and critical interest. *Mr. Sammler's Planet* received mixed response. Irving Howe reviewed *Herzog* as follows :

> One wants from Bellow's fiction, a novel that will not be confined to a single besieged consciousness but instead will negotiate the kind of leap into the world which he proclaims, to savour the world's freshness and struggle against its recalcitrance.

This novel is against the expectations of affirmation expected by Howe. Bellow is reported to have stated in a conversation with him:

> It is hard work, a book like that. Each word is very carefully weighed and connected, closely connected, to the man. The internal process of Mr. Sammler require the very narrowest attention. You have to see that he is never speaking out of character and that he never says anything simply for the sake of saying the thing, but what I wanted to create – I don't know how successful I was in this – was the thinking of such a person, never disconnecting the thought from the person, so that these things are not presented in the book as sermons, but rather as a monologue.

Monologue is extensively used in this novel. Sometimes it overshadows the tale. The plot moves closely according to the movement of ideas. These ideas excite the reader. The plot consists of the experiences of an old man and they are the subjective state of his mind. Mr. Sammler is :

- an observer
- intellectually sophisticated
- foreign.

Because of these traits he serves as an instrument of Bellow's indictment of contemporary Society. He resembles the old man in Yeats' 'Sailing to Byzantium'. He is a 70 year old widower and full of ideas influenced by Wells. During the Nazi operation of Poland he lost one eye and he lives in a New York apartment with his niece. He has the vitality and prefers using the third person and first person narration. Mr. Sammler voices the anxieties and uncertainties that existed in 1960s:

> Individuals like Sammler were only one stage forward, awakened not to purpose but to aesthetic consumption of the environment. Even if insulted pained, somewhere bleeding, not broadly expressing

> any anger, not crying out with sadness, but translating
> heartache into delicate, even piercing observation.

While lecturing at Columbia University he encounters an unpleasant experience. But he gains a sociological insight into this experience. He is not offended by the abuse of a student activist. He thinks :

> The worst of it from the point of view of the young people themselves, was that they acted without dignity. They had no view of the nobility of being intellectuals and judges of the social order.

Sammler encounters a black student and he rationalises his insult. He was found pick-pocketing in a bus. When he questions him, the black youth shows his genitalia and threatens him. He is struck by his mastery and ''mystifying certitude'' of the black. When his son-in-law knocks down a pick-pocket he is hurt. This attitude can be called ambivalent. Sammler fights with several youngsters whom he does not understand. Each of these tend to typify sex, crime, art as their driving passion. His widowed niece, Margotte, always discusses intellectual cliches like: the banality of Evil. She cannot even wash a tomato without getting her sleeves wet. Shula, his daughter steals the manuscript of Govinda Lal. Stealing is an act of lawlessness or becoming contemporary. His nephew's daughter Angela pursues endless variety in sex and this means to Sammler experiencing the age. Eisen is obsessed with Modern art. Angela's brother becomes everything and a homosexual. The inauthenticity of these characters are admirably depicted.

The inauthenticity of these characters arises out of their boredom of their day-to-day lives and they create myths about themselves. Sammler's contemporaries have become duplicates of:

> Paiutes – of Fidel Castro?
> No, of Hollywood extras.

Sammler thinks that in order to become great one needs models to imitate. So he thinks that his nephew Elya Gruner is dignified and sane and he is different from the rest of his peers. Gruner suffers from a fatal ailment and this gives him an opportunity to think about death. This novel becomes a search for the sources of stability and meaning in an immoral society. He affirms human existence on the planet despite its limitations. This is also evident in Sammler's conversation with Govinda Lal. They talk about the desirability of human settlement on the moon. It is a lengthy dialogue and is a part of the characteristic of a Bellow hero. It is part and parcel of his integral experiences. He is tired of Marx, Weber, Scheler, Oppenheimer, Adorno, Marcuse, Brown, Ortega and Valery. He reads only Bible and Eckhardt. The moon-dialogue convinces Lal about the conquest of moon :

> it is a rational necessity. . . if we could
> soar on and did not, we would condemn ourselves
> . . . as it is, the species is eating itself up. . .
> Much better the moon.

Sammler thinks that it is irrational and that basic problems will not be resolved on another planet because human dissatisfaction may be more intensive there. Even death-wish is not biological destiny. This shows that Sammler believes in cognizance and acceptance of limits as essential conditions for living without dissatisfaction. Too many desires also cause dissatisfaction. Sammler also believes that Soul and sense of God are essential:

> Is God only the gossip of the living?

The above is Sammler's question to Lal when he discovers that Lal is irreligious.

Sammler's sense of God is closer to Hindu view of God. Many Indian scholars have acknowledged this reason as the factor of appeal for Bellow and their "Bellowing" research. According to Sammler everything must be known to man or else he would tend to disbelieve. Like Kierkegaard's real prodigy, man will be able to

> carry the jewel of faith, making the motions of the
> infinite, and, as a result needing nothing but the
> finite and the usual.

He rejects the deterministic influence of biological order on existence. He prefers 'some order within'. This means that he would affirm life here and find peace here. He wants to be "willing as God wills". Later in the novel Wallace thinks that wealth is hidden in the waterpipes and breaks them. The whole house is flooded and this serves the comic interlude in the novel. So Sammler's affirmation is a personal ethic and it is sanctified by a faith in God. He resembles Herzog and he criticises "the modern religion of empty categories and the people who make the motions of knowledge". His tone is always affirmative, and positive.

In this novel, Bellow brings contemporary history to highlight Sammler's search for a rationale to live in this planet. Many people have decided that moon is a possible habitat to escape from the earthly problems. Many think that poets and writers are no good because:

> they get no evidence from modern literature that any body is thinking about any significant question.

Bellow regards his novel as an answer to this charge.

Bellow has raised the purpose of Art :

– "art must be understood as a purgation of consciousness."
– "art has something to do with the achievement of stillness in the midst of chaos."

Sammler believes in the above dicta and offers a meaningful existence which is authentic and acceptable.

Bellow's fictive method is influenced by :

– his creative anxieties
– writing as a mode of affirmation
– his concept of the role of the artist in Society
– his concept of human nature which is rational.

Bellow believes in the autonomy of self-seeking meaning in the framework of human destiny. Modern soul experiences :

– self-imprisonment
– poisoned autonomy
– ego-centricity

The results of living in the insulated world of self and the resultant shocks of coming into the world are experiences of Bellow heroes. Joseph, Herzog are indulging in futile searches. Sammler is relatively matured compared to other characters because he believes that belief in God is beyond explanations. His victim-heroes are: Joseph, Leventhal, Wilhelm.

His survivors are : Herzog, Sammler.

Bellow fiction gives insights into understanding of the self, and creative anxieties of a writer in contemporary society.

Questions

1. Bellow confirms affirmation in the lives of his protagonists. Discuss.
2. Attempt a character sketch of Sammler.
3. Write an essay on Bellow as a 20th century American Novelist and his creative anxieties.

4. Critically appreciate the moon-dialogue in the novel.
5. Narrate the theme and technique of Mr. Sammler's Planet.

Points for Discussion

1. "Bellow's use of Socratic irony reflects his anxiety to give credibility to his affirmation and to bring it within the realm of the possible."– C. Kulshreshta. Discuss.
2. Is there a Jewish art ? – Harold Rosenberg. Substantiate.
3. Bellow is a novelist of the Intellectuals–Maxwell Geismar. Do you agree with this view ?
4. He is possibly the most cerebral novelist of the current scene in the anti-intellectual camp of American Fiction–Max F. Schultz. Justify this view.

References

1. Lionel Trilling	:	Simplicity and Authenticity
2. Malcom Bradbury	:	The Victim
3. Richard Chase	:	The Adventures of Saul Bellow
4. Dr. S. Prakash Rao	:	Modern American Fiction
5. Northrop Frye	:	Anatomy of Criticism
6. Maxwell Geismar	:	Saul Bellow
7. Ihab Hasan	:	Radical Innocence
8. Alfred Kazin	:	Contemporaries
9. Tony Tanner	:	Saul Bellow.

Creative Writing

– Adapt a Screenplay basing on Bellow's novel.

– Narrate the story in Sammler's words.

13. ROBERT LOWELL

INTRODUCTION

Robert Lowell was born in Boston in 1917. In 1937 he was at the home of Allen Tate and during 1940-41 he taught English Literature at Kenyon College. He received several awards for his poetry. He was regarded as the best poet of his times and his life and career were filmed by National Educational Television. Thomas Parkinson records the following names for the post-World War II period :

- the Age of Panic
- the Age of Records
- the Age of Criticism.

Lowell's first book of poems was *Land of Unlikeliness* (1944). It was followed by *Lord Weary's Castle* (1946) and *The Mills of Kavanaughs* (1959). Allen Tate says of these poems :

> There is no other poetry today quite like this. T.S. Eliot's recent prediction that we should soon see a return to formal and even intricate meters and stanzas was coming true, before he made it, in the verse of Robert Lowell....is consciously a Catholic poet, and is possible to see a close connection between his style and the formal pattern.

Tate reflected the hope that Lowell was a best poet of America. Critics have paid attention to the following aspects of his poetry :

- Themes
- Catholicism
- Radicalism
- Violence

The themes of his poetry are varied. His catholicism has been called by Will Jumper as "three quarters anti-Calvinism....the radicalism is a curious mixture of Jeremiah, St. Francis of Assissi and Karl Marx; the traditionalism resides largely in technical detail....and the violence is both thematic and technical to an explosive degree." This is a balanced estimate compared with that of Tate.

TEXTUAL STUDY

1. *For the Union Dead*

Lowell declared that he was "a worshipper of myth and monster." His famous poem "The Quaker Graveyard in Nantucket" refers to its sailors as sea-monsters. This is a favourite image of Milton. Milton compared Dagon, the fallen angel as 'sea-monster, upward man and downward fish'. It means unspeakable inhumanity. Lowell always makes use of his patrician, class-conscious, hierarchical background. He wrote a poem on Eliot and hence critics say that Eliot was to Lowell as Vergil is to Dante. He was influenced by Eliot's talk on Dante wherein he said :

> the possibility of the juxtaposition of the matter of
> fact and the fantastic

Earlier he had mentioned about:

> the possibility of fusion between the sordidly realistic
> and the phantasmagoric..

"Water" is a strangely quiet poem. It has eight irregular quatrains in which a man remembers a woman on the coast of Maine. The images of shells and other beach creatures are provided by the poem :

> each morning boatloads of hands
> pushed off for granite
> quarries on the islands,
> and left dozens of bleak
> white frame houses stuck ...

and later he says :

> The sea drenched the rock
> at our feet all day and kept tearing away
> flake after flake.

The poet is creating contrast between illusion and awareness. In another poem of memory of separation and love, namely "The Old Flame" he says :

> In one bed apart
> We heart the plow
> groaning up hill –
> a red light, then a blue

as it tossed off the snow
to the side of the road.

The above cited lines are a mixture of sex and frigidity, the plow and the snow and the critics call it ambivalent. It is said to comprehend the universe of antinomies.

'For the Union Dead' is a tribute to the soldiers who died in the Civil War. It expresses the death-wish of the union. G.S. Fraser reviewing this collection of poems said :

The long-fish-like cars suggest
Shakespeare's monsters of the Deep
appetite preying on itself; the worst
slavery is not the oppression of the Negroes but the
blind appetativeness
of the indifferent whites...

Lowell said that in tnis poem "I lament the loss of the old Abolitionist spirit : the terrible injustice, in the past and the present, of the American treatment of the Negro is of the greatest urgency to me as a man and as a writer." It is an ode to the Yankeedead.

The Yankeedead was a Northern Counterpart to Allen Tate's "Ode to the Confederate Dead". The main intention of the poem was to state the conflict and not logical dilemma. It is thus rooted in the ambivalence, according to Philip Cooper. Lowell believed that "a poem needs to include a man's contradictions". He once told Stanley Kunitz:

> In life we speak with many false voices;. . . One side of me is a conventional liberal, concerned with causes, agitated about peace, justice and equality, as to many people are. My other side is deeply conservative, wanting to get at the roots of things, wanting to slow down the whole modern process of mechanization and dehumanization, knowing that liberalism can be a form of death too. In the writing of a poem all our compulsions and biases should get in, so that finally we don't know what we mean.

I have quoted this long quotation because it is a general statement by the poet on his art and craft.

Lowell says in "The Ditch is nearer" in FUD :

Our end drifts nearer,
the moon lifts,
radiant with terror,
The state
is a diver under a glass bell.

Apocalypse figures in his poetry as in James Baldwin's "The Fire Next Time." Lowell uses it at the conclusion of *Benito Cereno*, The Old Glory.

Lowell denounced all nations that have nuclear bombs, in his article in *Partisan Review*, in 1962. He said :

> No nation should possess, use, or retaliate with its bombs. I believe we should rather die than drop our own bombs. . . The sovereign nations are really obsolete.

2. *The Neo-Classical Urn*

"Night Sweat", according to Philip Cooper, is a cosmogonic myth. He cites from C.G. Jung's following books to prove the use of myths in Lowell's poems :

- C.G. Jung : Psychology and Alchemy (1959)
- C.G. Jung : Aion – Researches into the Phenomenology of the Self, transl, R.F.C. Hull, 1959.
- C.G. Jung : The Myths of the Divine Child and the Divine Maiden, 1963.

According to Jung :

the cosmogonic myths are, at bottom,
symbols for the coming of consciousness.

The turtle of Lowell's poem "is a conventional representation of Vishnu." It is an archetype of Jung. In *The Neo-Classical Urn*, the same archetype is used. Philip says :

> The mothering turtle of 'Night Sweat' is in 'The Neo-Classical Urn' both the brain and the multiple victim of her child, the boy.

The Neo-Classical Urn opens on these lines :

I rub my head and find a turtle shell
stuck on a pole,
each hair electrical

with charges, and the juice alive
with ferment.

Later Lowell writes :

Oh Neo-Classical urn, Oh nymph,
Oh lute,

The crippled last survivors of the poem are the victims of Hiroshima and they are like "the spiders marching through the air." The turtle image and its mythic value in the poem are significant. The poet uses the concept of Maya and the image of the bubble is used:

Colonel Shaw
is riding on his bubble,
he waits
for the blessed break.

The poet swings between the mythic and mundane in this poem.

Lowell has expressed with force and emotion, the Faustian myth of Science and its grotesqueries. He thought of fate and in this sense he is compared with Baudelaire who "saw things so disturbing that they almost kept him from making them into Poetry." His poems exhibit the following characteristics :

- the influences of J.C. Ransom and Tate
- Use of Hindu and Catholic imagery
- Boston and New England experiences
- obsession with the World War II
- bombing and protests against it
- themes of self-destruction and assassination
- pride in his family ancestry
- caricaturing technique and irony
- recurring images : the turtle. skull. dome.

M.L. Rosenthal calls the poetry of Lowell as the poetry of Confession.

Questions

1. Critically appreciate the poems 'For the Union Dead'.
2. Bring out the symbolism of 'The Neo-Classical Urn'.
3. Lowell's poetry reflects 'a basic instability...because of the incompatibility of the orders it accepted.' – Thomas Parkinson Do you agree with this view ?

Points for Discussion

1. One implication of what writers like Lowell are doing : that their individual lives have profound meaning and worth, and that therapeutic confession will lead to the realization of these values. – *M.L. Rosenthal*
2. I am not sure whether I can distinguish between intention and interpretation. – *Lowell*
3. He is entwined in the great issues of our age – *Thomas Parkinson.*
4. Eliot is to Lowell as Virgil is to Dante – *Philip Cooper.*

References

1. Thomas Parkinson : Robert Lowell 20th Century Views.
2. R.P. Blackmur : Form and Value in Modern Poetry.
3. M.L. Rosenthal : The New Poets.
4. Lionel Trilling : The Experience of Literature.
5. Wimsat and Brooks : Literary Criticism : A Short History.

14. ROBERT FROST : 20TH CENTURY POETRY

Robert Frost (1874–1963) is probably the most celebrated poet of the world. Kennedy described him as the best poet of "our time". He was the bard of San Francisco, California. He lost his father at the age of eleven. His father was only thirty-four years old and he died of TB. Frost realised that his family had the recorded history of suicide and insanity. This biographical point is exaggerated by some critics and they argue saying that this accounts for :

- depression
- tragic inheritance

in his poetry. His childhood was burdensome as he had to slog and assist his mother in running the family. In 1895 he married Elinor White. By 1899 he established a farm and lived on it, at Derry. In 1924 he won the Pulitzer prize for Poetry. In 1957 he was awarded Honorary degrees from Cambridge and Oxford.

TEXTUAL STUDY OF POEMS PRESCRIBED

1. *Birches*

This poem first appeared in "Mountain Interval". It is a popular poem of Frost's though it is not a representative poem. In this poem the poet subtly blends observation and imagination. The tone of the poem is casual and conversational :

So was I once myself a swinger of birches
And so I dream of going back to be.

This is a boy's recollection of his delight :

When I see birches bend to left and right
I like to think some boy's been swinging them.

The poet also produces special effects by mixing fact and fancy.

Observe the comparison of ice with glass pieces,
Observe the comparison of trees with girls on knees.
Observe the comparison of the country boy riding birches.

The poem is based on scientific truths, fanciful reason, and metaphors involving certain reminiscences. He is pragmatic :

Earth's the right place for love
I don't know where it is likely to go better.

2. *The Death of the Hired Man*

This poem is collected from "North of Boston". It is a narrative poem in the form of a dialogue. It is a dramatical poem and reads like an One-Act play. There are three characters in the poem :

– a farmer, his wife and a proud hired man.

The third character is suggested and he is not an active participant of the poem. The conversational tone and tenor of Mary and Warren makes the poem more authentic.

Warren defines home;
the place where, when you have to go there
They have to take you in.

It describes everyday affairs and the two points of view voiced by the husband and the wife.

Another important emotion in the poem is desolation or depression arising out of death of Silas. It tells the story of human pathos, solitude and emotional dependence. Frost's ability to portray unusual states of mind is evident in the poem.

3. *Home Burial*

This poem is extracted from "North of Boston". It has intense and tragic passion with a subjective touch characteristic of the poet's nostalgic reminiscences. The conflict between an urban and rural couple is mentioned in the poem. The lady is slightly snobbish of her urban upbringing. She is hysterical and considers her husband an alien to her social perceptions. The man always thinks of his child's grave which is visible from his bed room. The poet's own experience of his son's suicide has a bearing in the context of the poem. They are concerned with death as a fact of life or an ultimate truth. But they perceive them in their own idiosyncratic ways.

It is strongly suggested in the poem that the woman could be insane and unable to understand her condition. The poet brings out the universal truth by saying that man must adjust or perish or face a neurotic breakdown. Her neurosis or psychic breakdown adds a touch of realism in the poem. Some critics read in this character a replica of Jeanie, the poet's sister, who suffered the same poignancy.

4. *West Running Brook*

This is a didactic poem among the prescribed poems for you. It has other features like :

- dramatic quality.
- conversational tone.
- husband and wife conflict.

These are obvious features of the poem. A young couple settle on the farm next to a brook which strangely runs west instead of east. The husband comments about the quality of the ripple in the river. Yvor Winter does not think that this is a poem of any substance. The husband observes :

> It is this backward motion toward the source
> Against the stream that most we see ourselves in,
> The tribute of the current to the source.
> It is from this Nature we are from.

The wave is a metaphor in the poem. According to Winters, the wave suggests permanence in transience. The brook "can trust itself to go by contraries, the way I can with you and you with me."

5. *Departmental*

This poem is extracted from "A Further Range". It has a sub-title : The End of My Ant Jerry. It is a non-serious and humorous poem. It is a confrontation between an ant and a moth on the table cloth. The ant is called as he and he is curious. He reports to all fellow ants the news of death but does not really bother about the event. The funeral of the dead ant, Jerry McCormic is described here.

The poem is a satire on any form of regimentation or standardisation of individuals. The conclusion of the poem is oft-quoted :

> It couldn't be called ungentle
> But how thoroughly departmental.

The colony of the ants corresponds to the organisation of human colonies. At times the modern methods and standardised norms are burlesqued. Bureaucracy is condemned in the instructions about the burial and the dehumanising effect of departmentalisation are revealed in the course of the poem.

Though the poems prescribed here do not give you a proper conception of the poet, they are evidences of Frost's skill and technique of his poetry. He defined poetry as :

- "a connection of two things in the universe.
- beginning with delight and ends in wisdom.
- inclusion of mind and emotions."

About the poet, he says in his essay *The Figure A Poem Makes* :

- "the poet is essentially an accidental collector of impressions.
- the making of a poem is largely a matter of trusting luck
- the poem's logic is backward,
- the poet touches upon is the chaos he has lived through.
- the lucky poets may give out a clarification of life."

Frost believed in the fusion of form and content. He was not a believer in the saying that art should teach. He believed in endless experimentation in form and content. He said :

> the great pleasure in writing poetry is in having been carried off.

Frost's poetry has deceptive simplicity and the average Indian reader is content with the surface reading of his poetry. His lucidity and images are profound and have a non-denominational spirituality underlying.

Questions

1. Describe the qualities of Frost as a poet. Illustrate your answer with the lines from the poem.
2. Discuss Frost as a modern poet basing your impressions on the study of *Birches* or *Departmental*.
3. Bring out the experiments made by Frost in terms of form and content.
4. Write notes on :
   (a) symbol in Frost's poetry.
   (b) a poetry of isolation.
   (c) Poetic style of Frost.

Points for Discussion

1. The Secret of Frost's wide appeal...fresh vitality... – *Lawrence Thompson*

2. The tone of his poetry comes from his own life. – *Ezra Pound.*
3. Frost's work, like his life is built on paradox. – *Louis Untermeyer*.
4. Frost is a poet of New England. . .Like Faulkner he is a representative of his regional culture.

References

1.	Lawrence Thompson	:	Fire and Ice : The Art and Thought of Frost.
2.	James M. Cox	:	Twentieth Century Views.
3.	Dr. S. Prakash Rao	:	Modern American Litt.
4.	Willys Wager	:	American Litt.
5.	Sidney Cox	:	A Swinger of Birches.

Translation

1. Transliterate 'Birches' into any language of choice. What points do you keep in mind while translating a poem.
2. Make a check list of symbols of Frost's Poetry.

Theatre Arts

Adapt 'The Death of the Hired Man' for the Stage.

15. EUGENIE O' NEILL

THE DESIRE UNDER THE ELMS – TEXTUAL STUDY

Eugene Gladstone O'Neill (1888 –1953) is ranked as one of the greatest dramatists of American and European dramatists of Twentieth Century. His plays are subjective and some critics point this out because the genre is basically an objective study or portrayal of life. His father was an actor but he did not find this a source of encouragement. On the contrary, he was biased against his father professionally and personally. He even dubbed him as a melodramatic actor and did not rate him highly. This point of biographical criticism is specially important in the study and analysis of the complex and psycho-analytical play.

O'Neill experienced the sense of insecurity and trauma of childhood. He could not adjust himself to small houses and changed his residence frequently and find a big house to satisfy his urges of stability and security. This is cited by some critics as a reason for his plays being lengthy and experimentative. This is because psychologists consider size and stability as a manifestation of hidden anxieties of a writer. He changed and turned to various subjects for his plays to exhibit a mysticism which was highly idiosyncratic and symptomatic of 20th century Drama.

His personal life and secret marriage in 1909 and divorce in 1912 created frustrations in him. He went in search of Gold and toured Central America. The insights of this sojourns resulted in *The Emperor Jones*. He attempted to commit suicide on his return. He was on long voyages and lead a life of destitution. He became a writer and soon learnt that he was suffering from T.B. Towards the end of his life he died of paralysis.

He was influenced by Greek dramatists and his output was prolific. He wrote several One-Act plays. *Beyond Horizon* is the tragedy of Robert Mayo. *The Emperor Jones* dramatises fear. *The Hairy Ape* portrays industrial unrest. *Desire Under The Elms* is a study of human possession and secret incestual desires.

Theme and Technique of *The Desire Under the Elms*:

As the title of the play suggests desire is the theme of the play. The play opens and introduces the three sons of Emphraim Cabot, the owner of the Cabot farmhouse. Simeon and Peter desire to leave the farm to California. They also desire for freedom and gold and desert the farm. Emphraim returns with his third wife, Abbie Putnam who desires to own the land. Eben also craves for the same land because he thinks that it is the legacy of his dead mother. He nurses secret hatred for his father. The play is divided in three parts which are further divided into four scenes. The following are the characters :

Emphraim Cabot	:	The Owner of the Farm
Peter, Simeon & Eben	:	Sons of Emphraim
Abbie Putnam	:	Third Wife of Emphraim

The Scene : New England, U.S.A.

Part I

Scene I	:	Simeon and Peter decide to leave the farm. Eben hates his father because he had exploited his mother.
Scene II	:	Emphraim is away from his house for a long time and the sons think he is dead. Eben thinks that he should restore his mother's farm by owning it. He thinks that his father had over-worked her. Eben desires to have fun with a prostitute called Minh, first mistress of his father.
Scene III	:	Eben returns late night and wakes-up his brothers and announces the marriage of his father. Eben offers them 300 dollars each so that his brothers could go away to California. In return they will sign on the documents and sell their share.
Scene IV	:	Eben goes out to milk the cattle and rushes in to announce the arrival of his father's bride, who is half the age of their father (35). She is introduced as a lady of vitality and determination. She desires to own the farm and the house secretly. She surveys the area greedily. This fourth scene of the First Part

reveals the influence of Freud's *Totem and Taboo*. The acts of Simeon and Peter in insulting their father, the confrontation between Eben and Abbie are the strong points in evidence of this. Abbie is attracted towards Eben and tells him that she is not his mother. Abbie has strong hold on Emphraim and she married him for his wealth. Abbie and Eben develop love-hate relationship.

Part II

Scene I : After the lapse of two months, Eben and Abbie discover mutual fascination. Abbie seduces him but Eben restrains himself, and taunts her. When old Cabot arrives she lies and tells that Eben tried to molest her. Old Cabot tells her that he will shoot him. Abbie says that she can conceive a son for him on the condition that the farm will be given to her. They both kneel down in prayer.

Scene II : Abbie and Cabot are in the bed room at eight in the night. Cabot tells how he made his stony farm fertile at the age of fifty and says that he was sturdier than Eben. He thinks that God is like a stone and is hard. The wall between Abbie and Eben becomes transparent and they are obsessed of each other. Abbie rushes into Eben's room and kisses him. Eben returns the kiss to her but throws her back. Eben cries: Mother, where are you?

Scene III : Eben enters the parlour where his mother's dead body was kept. He points to lustful Abbie that the spirit of his mother is there in the room. Abbie announces that she would be mother and mistress to him. Eben is bewildered and confused but decides to take revenge of his mother by making love to Abbie, who has taken her place and farm.

Scene IV : Eben is satisfied that he could avenge according to his desire and feels that his mother has returned to her grave. Abbie is sure of fooling Cabot. Eben insults his father and bosses over him. Cabot thinks that Eben is foolish and drunk but he does not suspect anything.

Part III

Scene I : After an year's lapse of time the scene opens with an announcement of the birth of a baby to Abbie. There is mirth and the guests suspect and wonder whether the baby is Eben's. Cabot is happy and he dances proving that he is energetic. The baby displays the features of Eben and he is happy and gloomy.

Scene II : Abbie's lust forces her to smother her baby with a pillow. She sobs loudly and the old Cabot is fast asleep. Eben is ready to go and Abbie tells him that she has done it to prove her love for him. Eben thinks she must have killed the old man and that his revenge has been taken. But he is shocked to learn that his baby is killed. He abuses her and thinks this is a wicked plan to send him to the gallows. Abbie also thinks that she should have killed the old man. Eben goes out to call the Sheriff and feels that his revenge mission is over but is touched by Abbie's declarations of love for him.

Scene III : After an hour, Cabot learns about the tragedy in the house and the incest that has taken place. Cabot is full of contempt for Eben. Eben decides to suffer along with Abbie as he is the accomplice in the crime. Cabot leaves the cattle free and leave the farm. Cabot thinks that all this is due to his fate and that Eben is the instrument of God. He reconciles himself for the hard toil and decides to work on the farm.

> The Sheriff arrives and records the confessions of Abbie and Eben. The play ends on a romantic note and the criminals go to jail in a cart kissing and embracing.

The play is a dramatisation of the hidden and repressed desires. The characters are natural, dialogues are real and life-like. The main propelling force in the three principal characters is sex and greed of money and gold. The theme of the Play *Desire Under Elms* is mother- fixation or Oedipal Complex. According to Freud, it is:

> a manifestation of infantile sexuality in the relations of the child to its parents. It is a state in which a person shows excessive affection for the parent opposite in sex to him or her, and corresponding distaste for his or her other parent.

Usually, the daughter's excessive affection to her father is referred to as Electra complex. In this play Eben, is a blasphemous fool who has too much of affection for his dead mother and feels that her spirit is still in his room. This complex is carried over to the farm which was his mother's and he thinks that his father had stolen it from his mother. He even steals money and gives to his step-brothers who also suffer from the same complex and regard Abbie as a 'sow' and tell their father that they would 'rape your new woman'. This extreme situation is deftly depicted by O'Neill.

The mythical technique in the play has been admired by the critics. It means drawing parallel contrast between the past and the present until the past becomes a myth of the present. Art becomes universal in this manner. The great merit in the use of a myth as a background are:

- tradition is preserved
- It is passed on to the new generations
- it contributes richness and familiarity
- it contributes universality
- it contributes depth and meaning to life.

The mythical background to this play is derived from Hippolytus-Phaedra-Theseus legend according to Edgar F. Racey. This was also made use of by Euripides and other dramatists. The attraction of the step-son and the new bridal mother is the crux of the legend.

Correspondences between:

the myth	the characters
Phaedra	Abbie
Hippolytus	Eben

Modifications made by O'Neill : the murder of the child. This is done to suit the dramatic purposes of O'Neill. The concept of sin in this drama is the Freudian sin of repressed sexual feelings and the consequences of it. Besides this the types of sin referred to are:

- the sin of Emphraim's in illegally taking the land
- the sin of Eben in lustful revenge-seeking
- the sin of Abbie in playing the role of the mother and the beloved
- the sin of Abbie and Eben in unitedly committing the crime.

The puritan faith of sin and retribution is also mentioned in the course of the seduction scene :

- the destruction of Abbie and Eben for the incest and their punishment.
- the downfall of Emphraim for cheating Eben's mother and stealing it, thereby causing her to become a spirit.
- the death of the sinner and the avenger.
- fulfilment of the curse of Emphraim, the religious.

The unified dramatic vision in this work is achieved by:

- symbolic incest theme
- father-son battle
- the use of myth.

Another dramatic device that O'Neill uses is the presence of the supernatural or transcendental or even mystical element in the play. It is accepted as faith intuitively and it plays a crucial role. Some critics say this is an instance of use of telepathy by O'Neill. Clifford Leech says that:

> separated by a dividing wall, they should be constantly aware of each other's presence, should be sensitive to slight sounds or movement, is rational enough... We see the wall as a barrier about to crumble...it is on the naturalistic plane.

Another instance is Cabot's feeling that something is uncanny and wrong in this house. He seems to be aware of some romantic occurrences and goes to barn to find some peace there.

Characterization in *The Desire under the Elms*

Characterization is near perfect and successful in this play. The points to be borne in mind while studying the characters in the play are:

– the technique : conventional realistic techniques:

(1) vivid traits and personality

(2) dominance of certain traits : Emphraim's egoism. Abbie's sensuality

(3) grotesque elements

(4) complex inner lives : Abbie and Eben

(5) responses to stress of circumstances.

Symbolism in the play: There are different types of symbolism in this play:

- character symbolism
- setting symbolism
- incident symbolism.

These symbols communicate complex psychological and mythic truths about the characters :

- the Elms are symbolic of the setting. They symbolise the mother and dominance of the woman to the extent of playing the role of mother-mistress.
- Incidental symbols are those that suggest the Nemesis *e.g.* ; elms brooding over the house, the farm symbolises Emphraim's materialistic possession.
- the farm, according to Whitman suggest the life-denying 'sterility of the puritan ideal'.
- the departure of Simeon and Peter suggests the exile.
- the use of myth for:

  repression, revenge, inhibition
  passion, incest, love, hate.

- the use of supernatural.
- a sense of tragedy.

- oedipus complex as universal urge.
- use of pantomime.

All these elements are used to depict a domestic tragedy and some critics call it a melodrama. Cabot is a Puritan and his ideals are supposed to cause the tragedy. All these views are partly true.

O'NEILL : A CRITIQUE

He believed that: "some form of super-naturalism... may express in the theatre what we comprehend intuitively of that self-defeating, self-obsession which is the discount we moderns have to pay for the loan of life." According to Gassner, he used expressionistic techniques. He was influenced by Strindberg and his expressionist theatre wherein everything is possible and probable. He drew heavily from dream-play. They portray inner voices and hold that soul reverberates the universe. He felt unhappy that he was misunderstood and called a sordid realist and grim pessimistic naturalist. O'Neill was also called a lying moral romanticist as he himself says.

According to some critics he anticipated the findings of Neo-Freudians, namely Karen Horney and Erich Fromm. Freud viewed man as a victim of animal drives. He gave hope by saying that they could be sublimated for constructive purposes. But Neo-Freudians use the same insights and techniques of Freud but think that man is totally free and can create his own destiny.

Neo-Freudians believe in the following: An egoist

- is a victim of neurotic pride becomes inhuman like Hitler or Napoleon.
- believes in vanity and untrue self-image.
- like a tragic hero does not think he is real and imperfect.
- tries to achieve divinity.

According to some modern critics O'Neill took steps for the theatre of tomorrow. Sinister maternity is the problem of all times. Nietzsche dealt at length about the crime of infanticide. The play is also viewed as a clash of two philosophies: Puritanism and Dionysisism.

Questions

1. Commenting on the technique of O'Neill discuss the significance of the title *Desire Under the Elms.*

2. Evaluate O'Neill as an expressionist dramatist. Point out his merit and demerit as a dramatist.
3. Bring out various dramatic elements used in this play.
4. Analyse the character of Abbie.
5. Estimate the contribution of O'Neill to theatre.

Points for Discussion

1. He has transformed the American drama into a world of splendour, fear and greatness.

   – Sinclair Lewis.

2. American drama begins with O'Neill.

   –Doris Folk

3. He has experimented with a variety of dramatic forms and modes.

   – John Gassner

4. His characters are melodramatic in the sense that they are ''improbable and unrealistic''.
5. O'Neill is a dramatist of ironic fate and of tragic tensions, arising out of man's disorientations and man's bewilderment and bedevilment from within and without.
6. He has widened the range of our theatre.

References

1.	Robert Spiller	:	The Cycle of American Drama
2.	Doris Alexander	:	The Tempering of O'Neill
3.	J.W. Krutch	:	American Drama Since 1918
4.	Montrose Moses	:	The American Dramatists
5.	Dr. S. Prakash Rao	:	Apocalyptic Vision in Modern American Fiction.
6.	J.T. Sipley	:	The Art of O'Neill.

Creative Writing for TV and Films

– Write a Screenplay for 'The Desire Under the Elms'.
– Keeping the symbols in mind, what Art Effects would you provide for this play.
– Project this play as an actor's medium/Director's medium.

16. TENNESSE WILLIAMS : *THE GLASS MENAGERIE*

Introduction

Before introducing Williams, it must be mentioned that some plays of his are stamped with genius and some are trivial. He is highly individualistic in his choice of themes and techniques. He once said:

> you don't seem to see that
> I put my heart into this
> play,

Williams (1911–) was born in Columbus, Mississipi. Two incidents that affected his development as an artist and an individual deserve mention here. First was his altercation with a Negro nurse whom he called a Nigger. He developed a sense of guilt and much later abhorred discrimination. Second, was his suffering arising out of diphtheria. He got partly paralysed and contracted a kidney ailment. He became a subjective, introspective, isolated and a private artist. This probably explains why he delights in portraying a world of fantasy and reality. Another influence on him was his sister who was his 'playmate, confidante and symbol of beauty and fragility'. His mother was protective and a nurturer and his grand parents were aristocratic and protective. This explains why some characters in William's plays are overprotective, sensitive and delicate. Reading of biographical details into the criticism of an artist suffers from certain fallacies but not in the case of Williams. As an inseparable companion his sister supported him :

> Life was pleasant–gracious, full of imaginings... We lived in small Mississipi towns. We always had a large backyard...My sister and I played together. We invented games . The poor children used to run all over town, but my sister and I played in our own backyard. We were exclusive . . .My sister was an ideal playmate. My sister was very charming – very beautiful. She had an incredible imagination we were so close to each other, we had no need of others.

I quote this passage because it throws light on Williams' personality.

Such responses are recreated in *The Glass Menagerie* particularly, the somber, depressing and ugly apartment. He says "the apartment we lived wasn't as dingy and poverty-stricken as that in the play, but I can't say much for it." Rose's sunless room overlooked an alley which was a dead-end. She often saw dogs cornering and tearing stray cats to pieces. He says to compensate this his sister put "white curtains and tiny menagerie of glass..Somewhere between them was the world that we lived in." He hated his father for his hard and loud ways.

Williams felt alienated and wrote prodigiously in the cellar of Mrs. McBurney's house which he called as the literary factory. He read Rimbaud, Rilke, Chekhov, Wilde, Melville, Stephen Crane and D.H. Lawrence. The influence of Lawrence was profound and he wrote a play after him titled, *I Rise in Flame, Cried The Phoenix*. Chekhov's central theme of one civilization displacing another appealed to him as he saw in it the change of ante-bellum and Southern civilizations. Hart Crane influenced him in the perception of tragic intensity. He also took lessons from the theatre group called the Mummers. They were leftist rebellious, Bohemian and inventive. In New Orleans he found a kaleidoscope of sex, drinks and heterosexual revelry. He said "I found the kind of freedom I had always needed."

These influences fused the puritan and bohemian in Williams. His early works cannot be discussed without mentioning the exerting influence of D.H. Lawrence. His literary patronage extended to understanding of the sexual relationship and toward man in society. Lawrence had illuminated :

- the antagonism in sexual relationship
- the sterilization of human life
- the vital need to awaken the physical self.

He says :

> Lawrence felt the mystery and power of sex, as the primal life urge, and was the life-long adversary of those who wanted to keep the subject locked away in the cellars of prudery...all in all his work is probably the greatest modern monument to the dark roots of creation.

As a puritan he felt the repression and its consequences on his nature. He thought he was stultified by the mechanised and barren society.

In *Battle of Angels* Williams tells the tale of :

> a wild-spirited boy who wanders into a conventional community of the South and creates the commotion of a fox in a chicken soop.

Later he wrote, *Orpheus Descending* and *Sweet Bird of Youth.* He uses Christian and Pagan symbolism but some critics complain of operatic fiasco in the final Act.

The Lawrencian plot is obvious:

Val Xavier is a superficial, primitive wanderer with a virile grace and physical appeal. Val tells Myra:

Myra : Nobody gets to know anybody?

Val : No. Don't you see how it is? We're all of us locked up tight inside our own bodies. Sentenced – you might say – to solitary confinement inside our own skins.

Theme and Technique of *The Glass Menagerie*

This play reveals the influence of Lawrence and the view that he liberated the human soul and body. It is a story of "a son's need to break away from his mother and the awakening of a repressed female by a vital male." It is also most biographical of his dramas. Seven scenes comprise this play and portray St. Louis days of 1930s. It is called an uncompromising portrait of the tragic situation which was the home of Williams.

In this play, Tom Wingfield, a dreamy youth is bound to his sister and mother because of the desertion of them by his father. He desires to escape from them. He has to act without pity. His mother Amanda is torn between the two worlds of dream and reality. Her son is a poet with a job in the warehouse. His sister has withdrawn to a world of glass figurines which cannot be moved from the shelf. She is helpless and is lost, submerged in a world of imagination. She needs a husband who can provide for her. Tom brings a match for her. He works with him in the Shoe Corporation. Their relationship is incipient and Jim and Laura do not progress. She is like a figurine in the glass shelf.

Amanda is not able to turn the illusions of her daughter Laura into realistic events. She is a least impressive character in the play. She is beautiful and fragile but anachronistic in the world. She suffers from inferiority complex and mental unbalance. She is like a glass touched by light and her radiance is momentary. Jim arouses emotions in Laura.

And they share some parts of American Dream. Amanda is horribly dared in her mannerisms and dressing. She is puritanical and narrow-minded. She has heroism and endurance, and emerges as a noble, and tender figures with a valour. For her life is finally overwhelming. John Gassner says in a summary fashion :

> Williams retains a highly objective attitude toward his picture of a life of failure. He locates his story in the context of the larger world, which demands a wideawake attitude toward a society that ailing, and torn with the conflict of a Second World War, challenges our capacity for action. . . .The play is a mood.

Tom Wingfield, is the narrator of the play. He is caught in the web of the family and stifling job in the shoe company. He wants to abandon his mother and sister. Like Paul Morel of *Sons and Lovers*, he walks out of the darkness toward the challenging situation. Amanda accuses him :

> Go to the movies, go ! Don't think about us, a mother deserted, an unmarried sister who's crippled and has no job ! Don't let anything interfere with your selfish pleasure. Just go, go, go,– to the movies.

The strengths of this play are :

- delicate sympathetic, objective creation of meaningful people in a meaningful situation.
- portrayal of desperate moment in the lives of people.
- sense of deep meaning.

Characterization

Williams' characters are superficial and flat. They are of unidimension. The character of Amanda is multi-faceted. Pantomime is used in the climax because the power of words spoken is limited. Joseph Wood Krutch appreciates the delicate and economical characterization. But they are full of pretentious, sentimental, pseudo-poetic verbiage. The play is accused of using strained lyricism, and self-conscious poetic passages. The play has artistic and technical deficiencies. The weaknesses of the play lie in :

- core philosophy of the play

- tragic situations
- characters of the play
- world of illusions.

Destruction is implicit in the world of Williams. He says :

> The nature of man is full of makeshift arrangements, devised by himself to cover his incompletion. He feels a part of himself to be like a missing wall or a room left unfurnished and he tries as well as he can to make up for it. The use of imagination, resorting to dreams, or the loftier purpose of art, is a mask he devises to cover his incompletion. Violence, war, surrender of self are all compensations to cleanse one's self of man's guilt.

The above quotation is the core philosophy of Williams and offers illuminating commentary about himself and his work. It is derived from his short story : "Desire and the Black Masseur". Purification is sought through violence. The underlying belief of this play is that "there is very little, if any reason for living. Man is by nature incomplete because his Universe is fragmented. Nothing can be done about it. Human guilt becomes a corollary of universal guilt and man's life is an atonement for the human condition." Man is trapped in a determined universe. The pathos of such entrapment is portrayed in *The Glass Menagerie,* in an objective and moving manner.

Conclusion

This play was a success on the stage. In one One-Act play : "The Lady of Larkspur Lotion" a writer asks :

> Is there no mercy left in the world any more?
> What has become of passion and understanding?
> Where have they all gone to?
> Where's God?
> Where's Christ?

These questions reverberates Williams' work softly in this play.

Questions

1. Analyse the theme and technique of *The Glass Menagerie.*
2. Attempt a character sketch of Laura.

3. What is the narrator's point of view in this play.
4. *The Glass Menagerie* is a tragedy. Discuss.
5. Attempt a character sketch of Amanda.

Points for Discussion

1. The dominant theme of Williamss' work is the loneliness of human existence. Discuss
2. The universe is the great antagonist in Williams. Substantiate.
3. Man's life is a constant attempt to compensate for this lack of wholeness. Justify this statement of Williams.
4. This play has genuine artistic validity. Justify.
5. Williams is not a realist or a naturalist but his works represent a tenuous but taut alliance between harsh realism and a poetic – even lyric expressionism. Argue in favour of this statement.

References

1. Eric Bentley : What is Theatre?
2. Marya Mannes : The Magic of T.Williams.
3. John Mason Brown : As They Appear
4. Elia Kazan : *Notebook..*
5. Benjamin Nelson : T. Williams.
6. Dr. Prakash Rao S. : Modern American Fiction.

RESEARCH TOPICS IN AMERICAN LITERATURE

1. Aesthetics of Poe's works.
2. Poe's Concept of Art – Dostoevsky.
3. Theme of Death in Nineteenth Century American Litt.
4. Emerson's Orientalism : A Reinterpretation.
5. Nationalist Sentiments in Whitman's Poetry.
6. Mellville's Narrative Technique.
7. Twain and American Humourist Tradition.
8. Anti-apocalyptic Vision in Saul Bellow.
9. The Cycle of American Drama in O' Neill.
10. A Comparative Study of T.Williams and Oscar Wilde.

RESEARCH TOPICS FOR FILMS AND MEDIA COMMUNICATION

THEATRE ARTS SCHOLARS

1. Aesthetics of Films ....
2. A Comparative Study of Milton and V. Satayanarayana.
3. Translation of P.V Narasimha Rao's *Sahasraphan* into other regional languages.
4. *Rasa* in 20th Centuray American Poetry.
5. Indian Element in 19th Century American Poetry.
6. Literary Values in the choreography of Bollywood.
7. Phonetic anaysis of TV's Newsreaders – A Study in Intelligibility.

INDEX

SUBJECT INDEX